EVERY DAY
IS A
FIELD
TRIP

Escape Routine, Find Fun,
and Live A More Fulfilling Life

JAY HUMMER

SPARKLING I

D0841423

SPARKLING DAY PRESS

PO Box 68
Shrewsbury, MA 01545
info@everydayisafieldtrip.com
www.sparklingdaypress.com
www.everydayisafieldtrip.com

Publisher's Cataloging-In-Publication Data
(Prepared by The Donohue Group, Inc.)

Names: Hummer, Jay, author.
Title: Every day is a field trip : escape routine, find fun, and live a more
    fulfilling life / Jay Hummer.
Description: Shrewsbury, MA : Sparkling Day Press, [2021]
Identifiers: ISBN 9781736561805 (hardcover) | ISBN 9781736561812
    (paperback) | ISBN 9781736561829 (Kindle) | ISBN 9781736561836
    (NOOK) | ISBN 9781736561843 (ebook)
Subjects: LCSH: Leisure--United States--Psychological aspects--
    Anecdotes. | Pleasure--Anecdotes. | Quality of life--United States-
    -Anecdotes. | Travel--Anecdotes. | Lifestyles--United States--
    Anecdotes. | LCGFT: Anecdotes. | Self-help publications.
Classification: LCC GV14.4 .H86 2021 (print) | LCC GV14.4 (ebook) |
    DDC 306.4/812/02--dc23

CONTENTS

Part 1: Discovering Field Trips 3

   1: Yankee Stadium 5

   2: The Splinter 9

   3: Illegal Game 15

   4: Mental Health Day 19

   5: Southern Hospitality. 23

Part 2: Building Field Trips into Work 27

   6: The Road Trip. 29

   7: The Beautiful Everything 33

   8: Motivational Fuel 39

   9: October Glory 43

  10: Free Vegas 49

  11: Risky Ride. 55

  12: Labeled. 61

  13: Unforgettable Car Service 65

  14: Stuck 69

  15: Gruetzi 73

  16: Taste Bud Bonanza. 77

  17: Downsized 83

**Part 3: Building Field Trips
into Family Life. 89**

  18: Helen 91

  19: The Bus Stop 95

  20: The Beach. 99

  21: School Trips 103

  22: Band Trip 107

  23: Bad Day of Baseball 111

  24: Moosing 119

25: Fairway Friends 123
26: Sea and Air 129
27: Blueberry Hill 135
28: Determined to Play 139
29: Catching the Sun 147

**Part 4: Field Trips to
Challenge Yourself 153**
30: Yikes! 155
31: Fear of Heights 161
32: Split 169
33: Brooklyn Bridge 173
34: Rapids of Mayhem 183
35: Forty-Eight Mountains 191
36: Bucket List 215
Epilogue 239
Acknowledgments
About the Author

EVERY DAY IS A FIELD TRIP

PART 1

Discovering Field Trips

When I was a kid, a field trip during school hours was like a summer vacation—no schedule to follow, no desk to sit at, and no schoolwork to do. Just fun!

The Bronx Zoo was my favorite field trip. The live tigers, lions, elephants, zebras, and giraffes absolutely thrilled me. I felt transported to Africa, like an explorer on safari. What a total blast!

I also loved New York's Museum of Natural History. I still remember Manhattan's crowded streets and awesome buildings and the kids pouring out of countless yellow busses like they'd just been freed from a year of hibernation! It felt magical even before I stepped inside and saw whales hanging from the ceiling, exotic animals frozen in time, and giant dinosaur skeletons.

Back then, I thought only teachers could organize field trip adventures. But eventually I figured out they weren't limited to the school day, and I didn't need other people to make them happen.

What is a field trip, anyway? It's anything that shifts your perspective, fires up your imagination, shows you something new, or challenges your comfort zone. It's both the real-deal experience and a mindset for building more fun into your life. After all, adults need play, too!

This book will help you discover the everyday field trips around you—even if you have a stressful job, a young family, or a nonexistent budget. It includes everything from free, low-key activities to comfort-zone-challenging adventures.

I hope each large or small field trip boosts your wellbeing, connects you to others, and makes you feel like a kid excited by the prospect of a whole lotta fun.

Enjoy the ride!

1

Yankee Stadium

I didn't realize it at the time, but I made my own field trips happen at an early age.

They began in "The Woods," a small sandlot behind our house, where my siblings, friends, and I played everything from football to baseball to kickball. (Have you ever seen the movie Sandlot? That was us.) I lived for all sports, but baseball was my passion.

Where I lived in Stamford, Connecticut, local TV stations broadcast both the Yankees and the Mets. Whenever I could wrestle our one household TV from my siblings, I'd watch either team. But when my friend and teammate Danny invited my brother and me to a Yankees' game when I was eight years old, it was like Christmas had come early!

What I mostly remember about the game was the Great Mickey Mantle, one of baseball's biggest superstars along with Hank Aaron and Willie Mays. I often imagined myself as the famous outfielder whenever I sprinted and dove to catch fly balls in our sandlot. Now, the legend stood just a few hundred yards away. I felt complete in the presence of such greatness!

Sports heroes—like safari animals—were so much cooler in person. I just had to get myself back to another Major League Baseball game. Unfortunately, my dad was not a sports fan and had absolutely no interest in taking me. Still, I didn't give up on my field-trip dream.

Mickey Mantle had set my roots as a Yankees fan. But when Borden's put coupons for free Mets' tickets on their milk cartons, I went to work. Mom helped me by only purchasing that brand. I saved those coupons all year. When I finally had enough, my parents loaded the whole family into the car and headed to Shea Stadium.

But we couldn't get tickets—the game was already sold out.

I was crushed when we had to turn toward home and even more when I read about the game the next day. The Mets' Tom Seaver had pitched a no-hitter until the ninth inning. Just two outs from a perfect game, the Cubs' Jim Qualls hit a line drive. Qualls became famous for that hit—and the game went down in baseball history as the legendary "Imperfect Game."

And I had totally missed it.

I made do with TV games, but still yearned for live action—the energy of the fans, the crack of the bat, and seeing my heroes in the flesh. It took another year, but eventually I convinced Dad to take our family to see the Yankees play the Red Sox in a doubleheader.

Dad grumbled about everything—the traffic, parking, and crowds—but I couldn't have been happier!

We settled into our first base-side seats in front of the perfectly mowed, magically green field. The announcer's voice boomed over the PA system. Filled with thousands of excited fans, Yankee Stadium seemed larger than life.

Then I glimpsed the Yankees' "dirt-dog" catcher Thurman Munson, my newest hero Bobby Murcer, and the regal Mel Stottlemyre warming up on the mound. The Red Sox's Carl Yastrzemski, and the Conigliaro brothers, Tony and Billy, watched from their dugout. Players I'd seen on TV and read about in the sports pages were right in front of me! Just when the action was getting good, my brother nudged my elbow; our family was standing up. We were in the wrong seats and had to move.

Soon after we found our seats near third base, my brother realized he didn't have the glove he'd brought to catch foul balls. "I think I left it at the first set of seats," he told Dad.

Dad had to hike all the way back to the first-base side of the stadium to look for it, but no one had seen it. Later, we found it in the car.

The Red Sox sewed up the first game in only two hours and nine minutes, but Dad had enough. He just couldn't embrace a field trip outside his comfort zone—especially one that required multiple trips between the first and third-base seats.

"We're leaving!" he announced.

I was devastated to miss the second game.

Dad never returned to a Major League baseball game, but I did. I discovered some of my friends' parents would drive if Dad would buy the tickets—a win-win in my book!

Whether you're a kid or an adult, obstacles will get in the way of your field-trip dreams. But every obstacle has a work-around.

Can't afford Major League Baseball tickets? Catch a minor-league game and watch the up-and-coming super-stars. Not a baseball fan? Choose a different sport—football, basketball, hockey, soccer, tennis, golf, even NASCAR racing. And don't forget the women's leagues!

Every sport has its own culture, and every game is an opportunity to experience a tribe's vibe and watch a live-action drama where everyone—even spectators—participates in moments of greatness.

If a professional sports game isn't for you, check out the next chapters for smaller, easier ways to capture some field-trip magic.

As for the rest of you: what are you waiting for? Get off the couch and get to the stands!

FIELD TRIP:
Go to a game!

Field Trip Challenge: Try Something New! This list offers a tiny glimpse of the wide world of sports.

Baseball Leagues: Major League Baseball, minor leagues affiliated with Major League teams, independent minor leagues, National Pro Fastpitch

Call-To-Action Plan:
1. List of teams I'd like to see.
2. Ticket cost and availability.
3. List of friends to include.
4. Transportation plan.
5. Post field-trip review.

Football Leagues: National Football League, Arena Football

Basketball Leagues: National Basketball Association, Women's National Basketball Association, Big3, NBA G League, East Coast Basketball League

Hockey Leagues: National Hockey League, Minor League Professional Hockey, National Women's Hockey League

Lacrosse Leagues: Major League Lacrosse, Premier Lacrosse League, United Women's Lacrosse League, Women's Professional Lacrosse League, National Lacrosse League. Minor League Lacrosse

Professional Soccer Leagues: Major League Soccer, USL Championship, USL League 1, National Women's Soccer league, Major Arena Soccer League.

Rugby Leagues: USA Rugby League, Major League Rugby

Tennis: World Team Tennis

Ultimate Frisbee: Ultimate Disc League, Premier Ultimate League

2

The Splinter

Sometimes I consciously make field trips happen and sometimes they just happen to me—like the time I went to see the Harlem Globetrotters at my local high school.

I grew up watching the Globetrotters' world-famous basketball exhibitions on TV. Their theme song—a bouncy, whistled version of "Sweet Georgia Brown"—primed viewers for their dazzling display of tricks, skills, and antics. They played—and always defeated—the Washington Generals.

As a thirteen-year-old middle schooler, I couldn't wait to see these basketball celebrities in person. Even better, I organized this field trip by myself, purchased the five-dollar ticket with my paper-route money, and walked to the school. No parents, no siblings. Easy!

I went early to snag a front-row seat, but as I slid onto the bleachers, a large splinter slid into my back side. Ouch! Off I went to find the men's room to pull out the painful piece of wood. But I mistakenly pushed my way into the men's locker room—and froze. Only five steps away, the Harlem Globetrotters in their distinctive red-and-white striped basketball uniforms stood in a huddle.

Every face turned to me as I barged through the door.

"S-sorry guys," I stammered. "Didn't mean to interrupt. I-I was just looking for the men's room."

"No problem," one of them replied.

"Hey, little man, come here," another player said, waving me over. Inside the huddle, they all gave me high fives and low fives. Then I explained my predicament and their brows furrowed with concern. "Oh yeah, man, you gotta get that out!"

"Bathroom's that way," someone said, pointing to the stalls. "Take care of that splinter before the game starts. You need a Band-aid® or something?"

"No, thanks! Thanks a lot," I said, hurrying to pull the splinter out. I knew those players were getting ready to perform. They could've shooed me away, offended by my intrusion into their locker-room sanctity. But they didn't—they welcomed me and cared about what I needed more than what they needed at that moment.

The Globetrotters' kindness took my breath away. I couldn't help thinking: Those guys are as great off the court as they are on it.

Not only did I root hard for the Globetrotters from that day on, I became a lifelong fan of their superstar attitude. They made me realize field trips are not only get-out-there events, they're also internal, feel-good experiences. As Winston Churchill said, "We make a living by what we get. We make a life by what we give."

Why not build a mini-field trip into your day—and someone else's—by doing a small kindness, like the Globetrotters did for me? It's easy, it's fun, and it makes the world better for everyone!

FIELD TRIP:
Do something nice for someone else!

Field Trip Challenge: Complete all the suggestions below!

Give Up the Parking Space: So many accidents happen in parking lots because people are in a hurry. If you find a space just before another car, wave them in and look for another. Maybe you'll inspire others to do the same.

Call-To-Action Plan:

1. Choose a field trip from the list below.

2. Set a time frame to make it happen.

3. Repeat!

Hold the Door: Strategically slow down or speed up to get the door for someone else. Don't forget to do it again when you leave! (If the doors are automatic, simply allow someone to go first.)

Let Someone Take Your Place in Line: It's pretty easy to tell who's pressed for time if you pay attention to who and what's around you: those people hit the line and frantically look at all the other lines. Let them jump ahead of you!

Pay for the Person in Line Behind You: Seniors and young people who live on small budgets need help. But even if the person doesn't need your gift, they'll still be touched by it.

Return Shopping Carts: At a recent trip to the grocery store, I saw a young mom who had just emptied her shopping cart. I said, "I'll take that for you." "Thanks!" she replied. It was even cooler when her husband yelled "Thanks" too! I didn't need the cart, so I dropped it off at the corral. That way, it wouldn't obstruct parking spaces or worse, roll away and damage someone else's car. A few seconds of extra effort makes the world better for everyone!

Send a Positive Text Message to Someone Every Day: This is not only a great way to start your day, it builds great relationships. Send a simple "thinking of you" message, tell someone how they impressed you, or express gratitude for something they did.

Like Someone's Post: I love it when I see friends brag about their good fortune on social media. I don't feel like they're trying to be better than me. They're just excited to share their good news. Too many people feel like life's a competition. It's not. Be happy for others!

Write Five-Star Google Reviews: Please stop destroying people's lives with negative reviews! If an establishment is not up to your standards, either let the management know how they can improve or don't return. If it's a business you like, help them grow with a five-star review.

Write a LinkedIn Recommendation for Someone You Know: Think of someone you know who does a great job and tell their network. It takes just a few minutes!

Take a Photo: If my bride Helen sees someone taking a selfie, she'll stop and offer to take the photo. She knows a shot taken by someone else is so much better. People always appreciate a memorable photo.

Give Someone a Compliment: Tell the bank teller or grocery-store cashier what a great job they're doing; let the chef know how much you enjoyed their cooking; praise a co-worker or even your boss (hey, they're people, too!).

Speak on an Elevator: My kids have always commented about the conversations we've had with others in elevators. Trust me, this is a GREAT field-trip opportunity! Just face the other person, say hello, and ask, "How's your day going?" You just never know what happens when you connect with people!

Redirect Gifts: Is it your birthday? Ask people to donate to your favorite charity. Hosting a gathering? When people ask what they can contribute, invite them to bring a nonperishable item for the local food pantry. Planning a child's birthday? Encourage your older children to consider donations instead of presents.

Donate: If you're like most Americans, you have a closet full of items you don't use. Clear them out and donate them. Or research different charities and make a contribution.

Give Someone a Hand: Offer to babysit for a single mom; shovel snow or rake leaves for an elderly person. Look around for people who need help and be a superhero!

3

Illegal Game

This is a tale of three neighborhood factions: the kids, the parents, and the field-trip Scrooge.

Shortly after I met the Globetrotters, my parents moved to a new house on a street with two cul-de-sacs. My siblings and I quickly discovered its best feature: sports field trips right outside our door.

A massive group of kids met to play baseball between the two cul-de-sacs whenever they could. We'd play for hours—only breaking for lunch—returning as quickly as possible to play more baseball or other games like kickball or dodgeball. For my siblings and me, it was out-of-the-movies perfection.

Unfortunately, our neighbor in right field wasn't fond of our games—he was a field-trip Scrooge. "They're trying to make a playground of the street!" he complained to the police.

Four times, the authorities broke up our games and told us street sports were against the law. Technically, they were right. The city had an ordinance prohibiting baseball on city streets.

"But we're not hurting anyone!" we complained to our parents. "The only people driving into the cul-de-sac are the people who live here, and most of them have kids who play in the street."

Our parents agreed. They knew we just wanted to have good, clean fun. They also knew that fun kept us out of trouble. I'm not sure who organized the revolt, but we all decided something needed to be done.

Turns out the neighborhood had an association and the president's daughter was a baseball regular. The kids and parents met, signed a petition asking the city's board of representatives to amend the ordinance. "We're not asking for a total end to the ballplaying prohibition," I wrote to the city representative, "but only an end to the ban on streets with no thru traffic and no sidewalks."

We even planned a demonstration in the cul-de-sacs. About fifty people showed up!

I have no idea what became of our request, but I know we didn't stop playing. Neither should you! Whenever possible, champion harmless fun for yourself and others.

Some of the best field trips happen right in your own back yard. Round up some friends, gather some gear, and let the games begin!

FIELD TRIP:

Create or play backyard and safe-street games!

Field Trip Challenge: Learn a new backyard game!

Call-To-Action Plan:

1. Identify the next family outing or friends' gathering on your calendar.

2. Check to make sure you have what you need.

3. Don't own it? See if you can make it! Don't spend money if you don't have to!

4. Have fun!

Game suggestions:

Badminton	Hopscotch	Möllky
BattleChip	Horseshoes (rubber if in the city)	Ring Toss
Bocce Ball		Spike Ball
Corn Hole	Inflatable Bowling	Stickball
Croquet	Kan Jam	Trac-Ball
Giant Connect Four	Kickball	Wiffle Ball
Giant Jenga	Manhunt	

4

Mental Health Day

Thanks to my high-school art teacher, I discovered a crucial kind of field trip.

Mr. Pride was one cool dude—he walked around like the world was a really great place. I recall making two projects in his sculpture class: a self-portrait clay bust and a wood sculpture carved with awesome chisels and mallets.

The class itself was a field trip, but it got even better when, on occasion, Mr. Pride announced, "Mr. Hummer, Mr. Smith, you two look like you could use a mental health day." That meant we could leave for the rest of the class!

My buddy and I usually headed straight for the gym. If the Phys Ed class let us join a game, we'd stay. If not, we'd find a pick-up game at the college next door. We'd burn off some energy and arrive back at campus before the next bell.

Those unexpected—and glorious!—field trips broke up the school day, improved our mood, and made it easier for us to concentrate in other classes.

Mr. Pride was ahead of his time because research has shown many benefits to taking time off: we sleep better and feel healthier; we're more focused, more productive, and make better decisions; we're more creative and generally happier.

Yet Americans leave vacation time and sick days on the table every year. Whether we're on the corporate fast track or work for people who don't care about our wellbeing, we often try to squeeze a year's worth of relaxation into a two-week vacation.

Mr. Pride made me a big believer in mental-health days, so I encouraged people to take them when I led business teams. "You don't need to wait for me to suggest it," I told them. "Just take it when you need it."

Yes, we all need to earn a paycheck, but we also need life balance—time to rest, connect with others, and have fun. Work will always be there!

But, wait, where should you go, what should you do?

The possibilities are endless, of course, but in honor of Mr. Pride's sculpture class and the great lesson he taught me years ago, why not explore a sculpture garden? They're cool places to visit—some are absolutely wild (literally), and others are great, green spaces within city borders.

They also combine the best of two worlds with amazing restorative powers: art and nature.

FIELD TRIP:

Visit a sculpture garden!

Field Trip Challenge: Visit all the sculpture gardens in your region!

Call-To-Action Plan:

1. Find a sculpture garden near you.
2. Research cost and choose a date.
3. List of friends to invite.
4. Plan the details.
5. Do a post field-trip review.

NORTHEAST

Massachusetts: De Cordova Sculpture Park and Museum (Lincoln)

New York: Storm King Art Center (Hudson Valley)

Pennsylvania: Kentuck Knob (Chalk Hill)

MIDWEST

Illinois: The Nathan Manilow Sculpture Park (Chicago)

Minnesota: The Minneapolis Sculpture Garden at the Walker Art Center (Minneapolis)

Missouri: Donald J Hall Sculpture Park (Kansas City), Laumeier Sculpture Park (St. Louis)

SOUTHEAST

Louisiana: The Sydney and Walda Besthoff Sculpture Garden (New Orleans), The Kenny Hill Sculpture Garden (Chauvin)

South Carolina: The Sculpture Collection at Brookgreen (Myrtle Beach)

Washington D.C: The Sculpture Garden of the National Gallery of Art

WEST

California: di Rosa Art Museum (Napa Valley), The Fran and Ray Stark Sculpture Garden at the Getty Center (Los Angeles)

Montana: Tippet Rise Art Center (Fishtail)

Washington: Olympic Sculpture Park (Seattle)

5

Southern Hospitality

I'll never forget how Southern hospitality saved my college baseball team's field trip.

In New England, the fields are still covered in snow when the season starts, so we wanted to make a spring-training trip to South Carolina. Our parents weren't going to pick up the tab, so we stood in freezing temperatures selling raffle tickets all winter—it was worth it when we finally boarded the rented white passenger vans and headed south.

I was excited as we crossed the Delaware Memorial suspension bridge (a beautiful sight in itself), saw Philadelphia in the distance, and traveled through the Baltimore Harbor Tunnel. This was going to be an epic field trip!

That night, we stayed at a roadside hotel in Virginia. The players all went about having fun, while the coaches buckled down to work in the manager's room. The next morning, the hotel was loaded with reporters—our coaches had been robbed at gunpoint!

Fortunately, no one was harmed, but the robbers took all our hard-earned cash, even the travelers checks (the only safe way to carry money before the wide use of credit cards and invention of ATMs).

As soon as the local radio station heard our story, it asked listeners to help replace our trip fund. Though we were strangers, residents pledged enough to cover our lost cash, and a local bank issued new travelers checks.

"Southern hospitality really does exist," our manager told the local newspaper.

Thanks to those kind-hearted Virginians, we didn't have to head home that day. We continued to South Carolina and played ball under a warm sun.

Field trips are always a good investment, whether they're yours or someone else's. From the hard work it takes to plan and finance them to the experiences themselves, they give everyone an opportunity to feel good and grow along the way.

Let's put field trips within everyone's reach!

FIELD TRIP:

Enjoy a field trip while supporting someone else's cause!

Call-To-Action Plan:

1. Choose a field trip from the list below.

2. Invite friends to contribute.

3. Repeat!

Field Trip Challenge: Donate above and beyond the cost of whatever you're asked to buy!

Discover local fundraising events (golf outings, dances, auctions, dining, and other opportunities). Purchase tickets and attend.

Purchase booster cards from athletic departments and then go to their games.

Buy whatever the school arts programs are selling and then attend their shows and concerts.

PART 2

Building Field Trips Into Work

When I left college, I set out to find an occupation I could enjoy and succeed at monetarily. Sometimes that quest felt like a field trip, and sometimes it didn't.

But life is always about choice. What counts is how we adapt to the curveballs and obstacles lurking around every corner.

There are endless great things to do and see in our world—if we make the decision to enjoy them. A field trip is, after all, a mindset for having fun wherever and whenever you can.

Hold onto the kid inside of you, and a job doesn't have to get in the way.

6

The Road Trip

Neither of my first two jobs—grocery store management and insurance—turned out to be field trips
for me. So, I asked myself, if my passion, professional baseball, wasn't an option, what would be the next-
best thing?

Broadcasting was one answer.

I knew sports and could talk a good game. Maybe I
could land a big-time sports gig on TV.

That idea felt like a field trip, so I gave it a go and landed a local radio job as an on-air personality during hard-
to-fill shifts. I soon became the early morning sports guy,
then the midday DJ, the advertising salesman, and the
nighttime sports reporter.

Eager to break into a bigger market, I added an on-air
graveyard shift at another radio station. Working around
the clock for little pay was a grind, but at least I was making great strides toward my goal. Then a giant field trip
presented itself.

I was at my Dad's house when his friend Ronnie came
by. Ronnie was a Country Music singer who had turned
down a recording contract when he was young. I'd often
heard him wonder about what could've been, and that
day, he told Dad he wanted to record a couple of records.

"Hey, when your first one's done," I said, "I'll get it
played and on the top 100."

"How would you do that?"

29

"I'll drive around to all the country radio stations and tell them about your record."

I had no experience promoting records, but Ronnie thought I must be an expert because I worked at a radio station. "Okay," he agreed. "I'll cover your expenses—but that's it. I can't afford to pay you on top of that."

I quickly did the math: My current radio jobs paid next to nothing. I had other offers, but I could put those on hold. Heck, I'd only been out of New England once, and here was a chance to take a two-month, all-expenses-paid trip to see America. It was a no brainer.

"I'll do it!"

And that's how I found myself on the ultimate field trip—SOLO!

Starting out, I knew nothin' about nothin'. Back in 1984, there was no Internet. Cell phones and Global Positioning Systems (GPS) didn't exist. I just drove from town to town, knocked on the doors of every country radio station I could find, and asked them to play Ronnie's record.

Along the way, side field-trip opportunities cropped up: I spent a few days with a friend in North Carolina, visited my aunt in Florida while my car got fixed, and connected with more extended family in California.

Trekking across the country had many obvious benefits, plus an unanticipated one: it made risk-taking familiar. By the time I reached California, I had the nerve to cold call The Tonight Show. The producers wouldn't even let me in the door, but hey, I gave it a shot! Maybe I didn't get Ronnie on TV, but I did get his record played on radio stations across the country—and it made the top 100!

None of that would've happened if I hadn't come up with an unexpected field trip when I heard about Ronnie's big project.

What big project have you wanted to tackle? Start it now—you'll not only feel good, you may even discover new field trips along the way.

FIELD TRIP:

Take on a Big Project!

Field Trip Challenge:
Don't just start your project—finish it!

Call-To-Action Plan:

1. **Identify your project.**
2. **Plan the details.**
3. **Create a completion timeline.**
4. **Describe how you'll celebrate your achievement!**

FIELD TRIP IDEAS:

Train for and run a 5K.

Organize all your photos in a scrapbook or create a digital photo book.

Be an extra in a movie.

Write a book.

Train to do 25-50-100 consecutive pushups.

Speak to students about your career.

Participate in community reading programs.

Take on a project with a friend.

Declutter your entire house.

Write a book of poems.

Visit all fifty states.

Learn to sail.

Paint your self-portrait.

Rent an RV and explore.

Learn a new language.

Go on a week-long canoe or kayak expedition.

Run a charitable fundraiser.

Learn to fly.

7

The Beautiful Everything

My giant field trip for Ronnie made me realize I wanted to make more money than radio jobs paid, so I took a franchise sales job for the Century 21 Real Estate Corporation. What did I know about franchise sales? The same thing I knew about promoting records—nothing!

The company gave me the world—expense money, a telephone credit card, and the whole state of Connecticut as my territory—so off I went, eager for the endless field trips my new career promised.

But selling franchises turned out to be a lot harder than promoting records. After two months on the job, I was failing. A company vice-president told me, "Just get your prospects to come into the office and I'll teach you how to close the deal."

"Is that all?" I replied. "No problem! I can figure out how to get them in."

I already knew how to cold call. Heck, I had gotten a guy with an independent record label on the top 100 just by showing up. The One-Minute Salesperson said, if you help enough people get what they want, you'll get what you want—an idea no one ever taught me in school but made total sense. I converted it to "Jay speak": Just ask people what their dreams are and listen. Then show them how to get there.

Everything clicked from then on. I held up my end of the bargain—I got people into the company's district office. The VP held up his—he showed me how to help people achieve their business dreams.

I was on my way. Once I started learning the business, having success, and making money, work became really fun. Every day, this kid from the neighborhood took a field trip somewhere. Sometimes I drove to new parts of Connecticut, sometimes the company wanted me at its regional office.

You need me in New York? No problem—another field trip!

Going to Manhattan and eating at great restaurants was so cool for a guy who grew up without a lot of money. Once again, I felt like that wide-eyed kid heading to the Museum of Natural History. I was really living! My career was in motion, I had great visions for the future, and I enjoyed life outside of my job.

Just when I thought it couldn't get any better, work offered me a new field trip: flying to Orange County, California every few months. Not only was air travel a new experience, but Orange Country was the beautiful everything! People, weather, buildings, streets—everything was beautiful!

I always found a way to play no matter where I went. While other business travelers headed to the hotel bar, I'd go out to see what field trips the community offered. There was so much out there, I couldn't imagine traveling to a new place and not experiencing everything I could fit in. The field trips continued to multiply, get better, and include more people. I have loved every one of them.

Long-distance travel is exotic and exciting, but there's so much to explore in my own backyard.

I discovered unique field trips traveling to most of Connecticut's 169 cities and towns during my early career. I live in Massachusetts now, so I wrote down all the field trips I want to take when I have free time.

I challenge you to do the same: Make a list of places in your state you've always wanted to see. Then, when you need a mental health day or an excuse to play hooky from chores, you have a field trip ready to go.

FIELD TRIP:

Explore Your Home State!

Here's my list of future Massachusetts field trips:

Becket: Jacobs Pillow Dance Center

Boston: Isabella Gardner Museum, Mary Baker Eddy Library (and Mapparium)

Concord: Orchard House (home of Little Women author Louisa May Alcott)

Gloucester: Hammond Castle, Dogtown & Babson Boulder Trail

Great Barrington: Monument Mountain Reservation

Hull: Boston Lighthouse, Georges Island (Civil War fort)

North Adams: Natural Bridge State Park

Sandwich: The Bulb River

Springfield: Dr. Seuss Museum & Sculpture Garden, Springfield Armory

Worcester: American Antiquarian Society

Field Trip Challenge: If you've seen everything in your home state, travel to another one!

Take an inexpensive flight off peak, a train or a bus, or drive if not too far.

Take a sightseeing bus or walking tour.

Call-To-Action Plan:

1. Create a list of sites you'd like to see in your own state.

2. Make a list of friends to include.

3. Create a transportation plan.

4. Do a post field-trip review.

Visit city parks.

Find the best food, bakeries, restaurants, holes-in-the-walls, etc.

People watch.

Find the best view.

Visit historical sites.

Explore capitol offices or statehouses.

Take in museums.

Travel on public transportation and see more.

Visit local farmers markets.

Find the city's tallest building and go to the top floor or observation deck.

Find the city's highpoint and stand above all.

8

Motivational Fuel

By age twenty-four, I had finally found work that felt like a field trip, only took forty hours a week, and gave me flexibility to take a mental-health day if I needed one. I was truly blessed to find a career with perfect work-life balance.

Yet, selling franchises wasn't always a cakewalk. Since sales involves regular rejection, I had to find a way to power through the low moments. Thankfully, my company organized annual field trips—a.k.a. "conferences"—packed with inspiration. At one event, I saw the great Zig Ziglar reveal how to thrive in an industry filled with losing. His presentation not only fired me up, it hooked me on motivational speakers.

Some people told inspiring stories about how they achieved success despite extreme hardship:

Andy Andrews had been homeless and living under a bridge, yet he clawed his way out of despair and became a wildly successful speaker and author.

Chris Gardner—made famous by the movie The Pursuit of Happyness— slept in homeless shelters with his toddler son before becoming a stockbroker and founding a successful brokerage firm.

On a solo hike, Aaron Ralston dislodged a boulder that pinned his arm. With no hope of rescue after five days, he amputated the arm with a dull pocketknife, rappelled down a canyon wall, and hiked seven miles back to safety. His book Between a Rock and a Hard Place was turned into the movie 127 Hours.

Other speakers had less dramatic tales, but each one taught me something important:

Terry Bradshaw, the great Super-Bowl-winning Pittsburgh Steeler, reminded me that humor fuels the drive and hard work it takes to win.

Former Washington Redskins quarterback Joe Theisman showed me what deep preparation looked like: He spent hours learning about our company so he could deliver a rousing presentation to agents grappling with a recession.

Leadership guru John Maxwell taught me how to be a better leader when I was responsible for helping 223 franchisees build their companies.

These motivational field trips stoked my fire when I needed it most. They taught me anything can seem impossible until someone shows you it isn't. That's the power of inspirational stories.

Everyone needs a pick-me-up to tackle the obstacles on the path to success. Make time for field trips that entertain and recharge, so you can energize your drive and make big things happen.

FIELD TRIP:

Go see a motivational speaker!

Field Trip Challenge:
Take someone with you to a motivational event.

Call-To-Action Plan:

1. Research a motivational speaker you'd like to see in person.

2. Find podcasts, YouTube videos, or online events if you can't find an event near you.

3. List friends to include.

4. Make a transportation plan.

5. Do a post field-trip review.

Recommended motivational speakers and authors:

Mitch Albom	Kevin Carroll	Alison Levine
Cara Brookins	Jim Collins	Allison Massari
Brene Brown	Jon Gordon	Jeanette Wall
Les Brown	Robert Kiyosaki	

9

October Glory

After marrying a beautiful girl from New York City, I took her away from everything she knew and loved. My new job required us to relocate to Massachusetts right after our honeymoon. Both of us had to adapt to the change, but Helen even more so. She went from hopping the subway to having to drive everywhere; she traded city excitement for suburban quiet; she gave up good pizza.

That's why I'll never forget the October morning she called me at work. "Holy cow, Jay!" she gushed. "The backyard is amazing!"

She had just noticed the view outside our kitchen window. New England's October Glory maples blazed fire-engine red; other maples glowed pumpkin orange and canary yellow, and the oak trees glistened with copper and gold.

A big smile spread across my face. Helen couldn't get that field trip in the city! Sure, the few trees scattered around urban areas turn color, but the sight of so many trees clustered together is dazzling—especially when they're right outside your window.

Helen's phone call filled me with joy—and made me appreciate the gorgeous fall foliage even more. I became more determined to make sure I didn't miss nature's once-a-year color extravaganza.

Starting in late September, I book business trips in northern New England or in other locations with their own version of October Glory, so I can "leaf peep" as I drive around for work.

On weekends, I pack my schedule with other favorite autumn field trips: long bike rides on country roads; hikes in New Hampshire's White Mountains; family walks and visits to apple orchards and pumpkin patches; and, of course, quiet moments admiring the view Helen discovered all those years ago.

Nature's annual color festival is just waiting for you to revel in it! Work will always be there, but October only happens once a year. Take the time to soak in its beauty—and then share it with someone you love.

FIELD TRIP:

Plan now for a spectacular fall!

Field Trip Challenge:
Take a leaf-peeping field trip every day in October!

See my suggestions below for fall field trips.

Call-To-Action Plan:

1. Choose a destination with fabulous foliage.

2. Research lodging, dining, and activities.

3. Make a travel plan.

4. Do a post field-trip review.

NORTHEAST

Maine: Baxter State Park. When I want to get a head start viewing fall colors in late September, I run to Baxter State Park or nearby Katahdin Woods and Waters first.

Massachusetts: The Berkshires. Western Massachusetts offers many cool things to do while leaf-peeping from late September to late October.

New Hampshire: The White Mountains. Although named for the snow covering its mountains from mid-October through May, The White Mountain National Forest provides a tremendous array of fall color.

New York: Adirondacks. Very much like my New England home, the Adirondacks provide a vibrant palette of fall reds, yellows, and oranges.

Pennsylvania: Pocono Mountains. Leaf-peeping starts mid-September and peaks mid-October in this tree-covered 2,400-mile area connecting the northern, central, and southern regions.

Vermont: The Green Mountains. I'm a big Vermont fan and think just about everywhere in the state offers a beautiful autumn.

MIDWEST

Michigan: Upper Peninsula. This region has twenty-plus forested state parks with ash, beech, maple, oak, aspen, sycamore, and tamarack trees producing brilliant fall colors between three Great Lakes. Go mid-September to mid-October.

Minnesota: Great River Bluffs. Expect to see yellow maple trees, orange oaks, and lots of wildlife foraging hickory nuts and acorns while you wind your way along the Mississippi River. Season peaks mid-October.

Missouri: Lake of the Ozarks. The Ozark Hills provide a stunning array of colors including mahogany, russet, gold, and scarlet during peak season usually around late October.

SOUTHEAST

North Carolina and Tennessee: Great Smoky Mountains. This area has over one hundred tree species, so it has an amazing color display from early October through early November.

Virginia: Shenandoah National Park. Here the most popular activity is the famous 105-mile Skyline Drive—leaf-peeping at its finest for those who prefer the comfort of their cars.

SOUTHWEST

New Mexico: Taos Ski Valley. The season in the southwest starts late September to early October and offers the most vibrant colors along the Enchanted Circle Scenic Byway.

Texas: Guadalupe Mountains. Yes, there's leaf-peeping in the desert! Beautiful red maples grow on the shady side of the mountains, where the desert remains cool enough for trees to grow.

WEST

Alaska: Denali National Park. For the best colors, be sure to get there by early October.

Colorado: Aspen. Named after the aspen tree, this town offers a spectacular autumn experience from mid-September to early October.

Oregon: Columbia River Gorge. From mid-September to mid-October, see the golden colors of the Oregon Ash and the big-leaf maples' deep reds along this spectacular, eighty-mile gorge.

Montana: Glacier National Park. This area has two separate occasions to see color: maple, aspen, birch, cottonwood, and huckleberry leaves turn in mid-September, while the Larch trees, deciduous conifers that turn bright gold before losing their needles, change in mid-October.

10

Free Vegas

Las Vegas is known for being crazy and expensive. While I've traveled there many times for business, I don't have an outrageous Vegas field-trip story—at least not the usual kind. I never lost big at a gaming table. (As the saying goes, "The only way to make money in a casino is to own a casino.")

I had to attend a Vegas black-tie gala to accept an award. That would have been a big night in itself, but the company also gave us tickets to "O," Cirque du Soleil's original water show, which, at the time, was a big deal. I love theater field trips, and Vegas has some of the best in the world. Plus, a large contingent was going. How could I say no?

Once we settled into our seats, I realized I was exhausted. I'd attended conference events and client meetings, jumped into my tux, sat through the awards dinner, then dashed to the theater. The energy that had powered me through it all had suddenly disappeared.

To make matters worse, the theater was really warm. The seats encircled a giant pool, so the air had a humid, sauna-like quality. That didn't bode well for me. My eyes started closing. I tried to forestall the inevitable with the usual tricks: a deep breath, a shake of the head, the weary eyeball stretch. Nothing worked.

Cirque du Soleil's magic dazzled everyone around me, but my eyes saw a magic of their own. Lesson learned: Don't go on an expensive field trip if you can't stay awake!

Instead, walk along the strip and take in the eye-popping resorts. Each one has attractions—gardens, artwork, architecture, fountains—to reel you in. As long as you don't take the hook, you can enjoy hours of no-cost entertainment.

Or, get off the strip and explore other dazzling sights. While it's cool to play a hand of Blackjack or catch a show, you can also find fun activities that won't cost you a dime.

When I brought my family to Las Vegas, my daughter insisted we head to the Seven Magic Mountains—a free art installation—for a "cool" Vegas photo-op. I had to pinch myself: When was the last time your kid's big request involved something free?

Right then I became an instant fan of Instagram!

Go ahead—make the most of your trip to Vegas! Pack your schedule with free field trips that keep you on your feet. You'll stay out of trouble, hold onto your hard-earned cash, and—most importantly—tell a better Vegas story than mine!

FIELD TRIP:

Explore Free Vegas!

Field Trip Challenge: See if you can squeeze in ten of the attractions below!

OUTSIDE OF VEGAS STRIP

Seven Magic Mountains: Located seven miles from the Vegas strip on South Las Vegas Boulevard, this desert art installation features seven painted-boulder totems created by Ugo Rondinone. I'd been to Las Vegas dozens of times before I learned about this hot spot from my social-media savvy daughter. Capturing a cool post with these cool posts is must!

Call-To-Action Plan:

1. Identify free time on your business itinerary.

2. Plan your field trips. (See ideas below.)

3. Consider if you want to include colleagues or clients.

4. Pack the right gear.

5. Do a post field-trip review.

Red Rock Canyon National Conservation Area. This stretch of the Mojave Desert offers one of my favorite free-Vegas activities—a 4.6-mile hike to the summit of Turtlehead Peak. But dress appropriately! One colleague thought the hike would be super easy and showed up wearing brand new loafers. After climbing nearly 2,000 feet of elevation, his feet were covered in blisters. Ouch.

Hoover Dam and Hoover Dam Bypass Bridge: Located about forty-five minutes from Las Vegas, the Hoover Dam is a construction marvel built during the Great Depression. The concrete arch-gravity dam sits on the Nevada-Arizona border and spans the Colorado River's Black Canyon. At nine hundred feet, the Mike O'Callaghan-Pat Tillman Bypass Bridge is the second tallest bridge in the United States. While it's free to walk across the dam and the bridge, there is a fee to park.

ON OR NEAR THE VEGAS STRIP

"Welcome to Fabulous Las Vegas" Sign: The sign was officially added to the National Register of Historic Places and has its own parking lot. Another Instagram must.

The Park Las Vegas: Near the T-Mobile Arena, this urban park features a forty-foot-tall Bliss Dance sculpture and fountains.

Water Features at Aria: No need to go into the hotel—the water features are near the entrance. Lumia's neon-colored fountains twist into ribbons and project large arcs of streaming water. "Focus" is an expansive, curved water wall of highly-textured stone.

Flamingo Wildlife Habit: A habitat of beautiful flamingos, birds, swans, ducks, koi, turtles and pelicans.

Circus Circus Midway: World-class circus acts daily.

The Chandelier and Street Art Murals at the Cosmopolitan: This dazzling chandelier is three stories high, houses three bars, and has two million shimmering crystals. For a less formal vibe, head to the hotel's parking garage and check out the cool street art murals.

The Bellagio Conservatory and Botanical Gardens: The resort casinos are so over the top, people often experience sensory overload and become oblivious to the spectacular surroundings. But don't miss this spot. The effort and talent that goes into these gardens is amazing.

Fountains of Bellagio: Visit these jets of water choreographed to popular and classic music. I promise you'll love it!

Streetmosphere at the Venetian Grand Canal Shoppes:
Browse the shops, watch couples share gondola rides in the mini Venetian canals, and enjoy singers, jugglers, performers, and living statues around St. Mark's Square.

Mirage Volcano: Experience these thrilling fireballs and explosions three times daily.

The Wynn Las Vegas: See the floral hot air balloon and carousel—you won't believe the number of flowers! And check out the Jeff Koons's Popeye and Tulips sculptures. Steve Wynn paid over sixty million dollars so the world could see these works at his resort.

DOWNTOWN LAS VEGAS

Fremont Street Experience: Viva Vision is a spectacular display of lights, technology, and street performers. You can also find downtown street art nearby.

The Flaming Praying Mantis: In downtown Container Park, this statue shoots flames that reach six stories high.

Gold and Silver Pawn Shop: Home of the television show Pawn Stars. This may cost you if you find something you like!

11

Risky Ride

Work events can lead to cool field trips—especially if your coworkers are game for adventure.

I was once at a corporate event in Savannah, Georgia, where the cocktails were flying. I wasn't drinking but was having a good time talking to my colleague Michael about how the first Formula 1 race in America took place in Savannah.

"In fact, just behind the hotel is an abandoned racetrack known as the 'Grand Prize of America,'" I told him. "That's where the race was held."

"No kidding?" Michael remarked. "We should check it out while we're here."

"How 'bout now?" I asked. I really wanted to drive on that track, so my mind was already busy planning a field trip.

"Now? You serious?"

"Yeah! Let's head over there in my rental car. We can check out the track and see what it feels like to open up the Infinity on the straight-away."

"Is that legal?"

"I suppose we could get bagged for trespassing or speeding. But I've seen the entrance—it's pretty desolate. I doubt anyone will see us. I'll drive, and if anything happens, it'll all be on me. I'm willing to risk a little trouble if you are. I mean, how often do you get to drive on a historic Formula 1 racetrack?"

"When you put it that way, we don't have a choice," Michael said, setting his drink down on a nearby table. "I'm in!"

Two other guys overheard our plan and didn't hesitate to put their lives in my nonprofessional driving hands. I guess they trusted me because I hadn't been drinking!

The four of us snuck out of the corporate event, secured our wheels from the valet, and headed for the track. On our first lap, we discovered the roadway is 1.965 miles long and has ten turns; structurally, it's more suited for a sports car with real handling capabilities—unlike my rental.

I went as fast as I could without risking flipping the car. With the track's relatively short straight-aways and four men on board, I was barely able to hit ninety miles an hour before having to slow down for a turn. Not exactly Formula 1 speeds, but we still whooped it up until after the second lap, when we decided to end the joyride before our luck ran out.

(I later found out the track was a public road, which explains why we could get on it in the first place. Learning we didn't trespass made me feel even better about our adventure.)

What a field trip! When I pulled the rental up to the hotel entrance and gave it back to the valet, I felt like the great Mario Andretti handing the car to the pit crew.

Buzzed from the adrenaline rush—we had conquered the track!— we returned to the cocktail party like victors and continued to whoop it up for the rest of the night.

Eager to unleash your inner speed demon? Head to the Grand Prize of America Road Course—it's still a public road—or find other speedways that offer safe, legal opportunities to drive like a pro!

FIELD TRIP:

Live your driving dream!

Field Trip Challenge:
Try all three types of
driving experiences below!

VENUES
FOR RACING
EXPERIENCES

Exotics Racing: Race Ferraris
at tracks in Las Vegas and Los
Angeles.

Call-To-Action Plan:

1. **Find a driving experience
   near you.**
2. **Invite others.**
3. **Plan transportation.**
4. **Do a post field-trip review.**

Indy Racing Experience: Drive Indy cars at the Indy 500
Track in Indianapolis, Indiana.

Mario Andretti Racing Experience: Fourteen tracks across the
country.

Racing Adventures: Drive super and exotic cars in Phoenix,
Las Vegas, Los Angeles, and Houston.

Xtreme Xperience: Drive exotic cars at their home track in
New Orleans or at one of thirty-five tracks across the country
during their tour.

TRACKS WHERE YOU CAN DRIVE
YOUR OWN CAR:

NORTHEAST

Lakeville, Connecticut: Lime Rock Park.

Long Pond, Pennsylvania: Pocono Raceway

Millville, New Jersey: New Jersey Motorsports park

Ware, Massachusetts: Palmer Motorsports Park

Watkins Glen, New York: Watkins Glen

MIDWEST

Elkhart Lake, Wisconsin: Road America

Lexington, Ohio: Mid-Ohio Sports Car Course

Mount Meridian, Indiana: Putnam Park Road Course

SOUTHEAST

Alton, Virginia: Virginia International Raceway

Braselton, Georgia: Road Atlanta

SOUTHWEST

Austin, Texas: Circuit of the Americas

La Junta, Colorado: La Junta Raceway

WEST

Monterey, California: Laguna Seca

Rosamond, California: Willow Springs International

Sonoma, California: Sonoma Raceway

Willows, California: Thunderhill Raceway Park

TRACKS WHERE YOU CAN HAVE NASCAR DRIVING EXPERIENCES:

NORTHEAST

Dover, Delaware: Dover International Speedway

Loudon, New Hampshire: New Hampshire Motor Speedway

MIDWEST

Joliet, Illinois: Chicagoland Speedway

Brooklyn, Michigan: Michigan International Raceway

Kansas City, Kansas: Kansas Speedway

SOUTHEAST

Atlanta, Georgia: Motor Speedway

Charlotte, North Carolina: Charlotte Motor Speedway

Daytona, Florida: Daytona International Speedway

Lincoln, Alabama: Talladega Superspeedway

Miami, Florida: Homestead Miami Speedway

Myrtle Beach, South Carolina: Myrtle Beach Speedway

Richmond, Virginia: Richmond International Raceway

Sparta, Kentucky: Kentucky Speedway

SOUTHWEST

Fort Worth, Texas: Texas Motor Speedway

Las Vegas, Nevada: Las Vegas Motor Speedway

Phoenix, Arizona: ISM Raceway

WEST

Fontana, California: Auto Club Speedway

12

Labeled

I f your company ever offers a self-discovery field trip, take it!

My colleague Chuck took a company-sponsored course called "Powerful Living" and suggested I enroll. But I wasn't sold, so Michael, the program leader, invited me to breakfast to change my mind.

"The course is designed to help participants get out of their own way," he said.

I didn't think I was in my own way: I was successful in my chosen career, had a loving bride and three wonderful children, good relationships with my Mom and siblings, and a beautiful home.

"I'm not a candidate for the course," I said. "I don't have any issues."

"Oh, you have issues," he replied. "And I'll find them."

I couldn't resist his challenge, so I signed up.

The program took place at Michael's home. When I arrived, signs at the front door directed me to enter through the mudroom door next to the garage. Once inside, I was told to take off my shoes and wait with the seven other participants in the family room while Michael and his team finished prepping. All of this seemed weird.

When we were finally ushered into the living room, I was surprised to see the furniture pushed back.

"Please sit in a circle on the floor," Michael told us.

Good thing my socks don't have holes, I thought.

Someone handed us printed labels saying "successful," "unsuccessful," "educated," "uneducated," "competent," "incompetent," "trustworthy," "untrustworthy," "friendly," and "unfriendly."

"Put the labels on the participants who match the category," Michael instructed.

I now realized those first twenty minutes had been a set-up. We'd have to base our judgments strictly on looks and waiting-room interactions. Can you imagine tagging people you had just met as "incompetent" or "unfriendly"?

After a few minutes, I had thirteen labels stuck on my shirt: successful (5), educated (4), competent (2), incompetent (1), and untrustworthy (1).

Then Michael started reading everyone's course questionnaires out loud. As I learned more about the others, I understood the labeling exercise. We pass judgment on people we don't know every day. We incorrectly assume who they are and what's happening in their world.

I not only learned how I misjudged others, I discovered what I put out to the world. Although I wanted people to see me as successful, educated, and competent, when I noticed others were considered "trustworthy" and "friendly," I knew I was chasing the wrong things.

WOW.

Night one, and I already realized I had plenty getting in my way. For example, I learned that while I love connecting with people, my conversation habits often undermined that goal. Whenever someone shared something I could relate to, I jumped in to tell my story. I wanted to point out what we had in common, but instead, interrupted and made their story about me.

I also struggled with being the "Answer Man." I tended to offer solutions when the other person really needed me to just listen and empathize.

The Powerful Living field trip taught me so much, I eventually became a coach. Amazingly, I found—and re-moved—other obstacles in my path. During one program, a single question unearthed a troubling past experience I had never addressed: Was there a time when someone took advantage of you?

The exercise was designed to help the participants for-give, not so the perpetrator could be absolved, but so the victim could jettison their emotional baggage and move on.

I immediately knew my answer—and that surprised me.

When I was sixteen, I was in a car with a close friend who drove way too fast and crashed into the trees, nearly killing us both. He took me on his high-speed field trip without asking my permission. Now I realized how deeply I resented that. I had never forgiven him for risking my life.

Two things happened after that exercise. First, I forgave my friend, invited him to a New England Patriots game, and explained how that experience had hindered our re-lationship. I'm happy to say, we moved forward and have had some great times since.

Second, I realized I may have made others feel uncom-fortable because I, too, like to drive fast. I still have to remind myself to control my speed, even and especially when my wife and kids are in the car. Just because they're family, I can't assume it's okay to drive however I want.

Field trips involving others always require permission slips.

I had thought I didn't need a self-discovery field trip, but I was wrong. I learned inward journeys are just as life-altering as outward ones—and footwear is entirely op-tional!

There are tons of programs and workshops to help you figure out what's getting in your way. Find one and jump in!

FIELD TRIP:

Take a life course!

Call-To-Action Plan:

1. Research life courses near you.
2. Participate fully—even if it feels uncomfortable!
3. Do a post field-trip review.

Field Trip Challenge: Create your own self-discovery field trip by doing the exercises below. You'll get a jump start on the learning you'll experience in the course.

Write a poem entitled "My Original Face." Who were you as a child, before people started to change you? Before you started to change you? What have you become? Don't hold back; reach deep to reap powerful insights.

Write your own eulogy. This exercise makes you realize if you've been living the life you really want to live. Are you making any type of impact on this world? Will you be happy when you leave?

Write the script for the rest of your life. Do this after you write the eulogy. Then follow it to create the life you really want.

13

Unforgettable Car Service

Traveling is the ultimate field trip, but many people focus exclusively on the destination. I've found cab rides can be adventures in themselves. My favorite of all time took place in Chicago. It was short—no more than half a mile—so I didn't have time to chat up the driver and catch his name, which is a shame. NASCAR legend Jimmie Johnson had nothing on that guy!

The cabbie fish-tailed—tires screaming—out of the hotel entrance then gunned through a yellow light at seventy miles an hour. Seconds later, he sped through a U-turn at what felt like forty MPH and screeched to a halt in front of the restaurant.

I thought, WOW, is this guy a stunt driver? Am I on some prank TV show?

As I handed over the fare, I glanced around for hidden cameras, half-expecting the cabbie to say, "You've been punk'd, man!" Instead, he just peeled out.

YAHOO! Pumped with adrenaline, I practically hopped to my meeting.

Obviously, I have a pretty wide comfort zone when it comes to cars and speed, yet I do have limits. On a cab ride from Istanbul airport to a resort about a hundred miles away, the driver pushed his small economy car up to 120 MPH. As we zoomed past other cars, I started to worry: This car isn't designed for high speed. It doesn't have the right brakes. If we stop too quickly, the guy behind us will crush me like a bug. Why am I trusting this guy with my life?!

"Hey, can you slow down??"

The driver ignored me at first. He was on his own field trip and hadn't asked if I wanted to come along.

I leaned forward and pointed to the odometer. "Too fast!" I said, shaking my head and frowning.

He eased off to about 100 MPH. I nodded and sat back until we arrived safely at the resort.

On yet another business trip, I discovered that sometimes all it takes to turn an ordinary ride into a memorable experience is a deeply touching story—like the one I heard from a seventy-two-year-old limo driver. He had grown up with a state-appointed name in an orphanage and worked on state-run farms. When he entered the service, he renamed himself Teddy after a teacher who had been the only nice person in his life.

Teddy spent fourteen months as a prisoner in the Korean War. When he left the POW camp, he weighed 100 pounds and was covered with more than 500 sores. During the two years he spent recovering in the hospital, he fell in love with his nurse. They were married for fifty-one years.

"She passed away four months ago," Teddy told me. "I can't sleep at night, so I might as well work. Driving gets me out of the house."

"I'm sorry," I said. "It must be tough."

"Yeah," he sighed. "I was lucky enough to know my wife, let alone be married to her."

That magical statement made me realize stories, like cars, transport us to different places and connect us to each other.

In honor of Teddy and his bride, make your next field trip about giving back to people who have spent a lifetime giving to others.

FIELD TRIP:

Give your time, meet new people, and create new stories!

Field Trip Challenge:
Acknowledge someone for their extraordinary service.

FIELD TRIP SUGGESTIONS:

Call-To-Action Plan:

1. Choose a field trip from the list below or create your own.
2. Invite others to participate.
3. Commit to a date.
4. Plan details.
5. Do a post field-trip review.

Visit the elderly and listen to their stories.

Cook and serve meals to homeless vets.

Build houses for Habitat for Humanity.

Volunteer for the Red Cross.

Volunteer in hospitals: help transport patients, deliver flowers, socialize with patients.

Teach life skills (job, parenting, managing finances) at a homeless shelter.

Be a Big Brother or Big Sister.

Help an elderly neighbor clean their yard.

Coach, train, officiate, organize events, or fundraise for the Special Olympics.

Volunteer in local libraries.

Compete in The Susan B. Komen Race for the Cure.

Participate in Easter Seals volleyball events.

Help maintain trails for national and state parks.

14

Stuck

For me, fitness is a field trip. It feels good to challenge myself physically and sweat off some energy. But once, while traveling, I perspired more on the elevator ride from the gym than during my workout.

I had checked into a hotel in Texas several hours before I had to attend my first conference event. After satisfying my dire need for Tres Leches cake at a local Mexican restaurant, I worked off the meal at the gym then headed back to my room.

On the way up, the elevator stopped, and fire alarms went off at full steam. I'd been stuck in elevators many times, so I wasn't unnerved until I saw the smoke. Not one to panic, I decided to call for help. Like everyone else, I always carry my mobile phone—except when I work out at a hotel.

Good news—there was an elevator phone! Bad news— no one answered.

Next, I tried to pry open the doors. They locked after two inches, but I could see I was stuck between two floors. If I could open the doors enough to squeeze out, I could climb to the top of the elevator and then to the floor above me. But as I struggled to widen the opening, I thought: What if the elevator starts moving while I'm only half-way out? It was a needless worry—the doors wouldn't budge.

I tried the phone again. I didn't think anyone was going to answer, but after several rings, a man finally picked up. He spoke in broken English, his voice was so rushed and nervous, I had trouble understanding him. He probably just wanted out of the building, too, but was stuck manning the phones until all the guests had exited.

"I'm stuck in the elevator," I explained calmly.

"Sir, there's a fire in the hotel. We need you to leave the building."

"I would like to leave the building, but I'm stuck in the elevator."

"You need to use the stairs."

Click.

At that point, I started to wonder if my fun, active life would end in this small, confined place. I didn't have any breathing issues yet, so was confident I could still figure out how to escape.

I looked up at the ceiling for a door. On TV, people always climb out through the top of the elevator and hoist themselves up to the next floor. I could do that, but there was no door.

I tried the phone again. Maybe I'll get lucky and someone different will answer.

"Front desk."

It was my friend.

"Hi again, I really could use someone's help as I'm stuck in the elevator."

"Sir, you need to get out of the elevator, take the stairs, and exit the building."

"Sir, I really need you to listen to me for one moment," I replied, my voice stern. "Can you do that?"

"Yes."

"I'm stuck in the elevator. It's not moving. It's filled with smoke. I would really like to get out so I can use your stairs and exit this building. But I can't."

"Okay. I'll get help."

"Thank you!"

A few minutes later, my friend called back. "The fire department is in the building. They'll come find you."

About five minutes later, a fireman spotted me through the two-inch opening I'd maintained to keep fresh air in the elevator car. I was so happy to see those guys!

"Everything is fine—there's no fire," a fireman told me right away. "The elevator belts broke. When they break, they smoke. It'll take twenty to thirty minutes to get you out, but don't worry about fire or additional smoke. You're gonna be fine."

I relaxed.

When I finally came down to the lobby with my new friends from the Frisco Fire Department, the hotel guests had already come back in. A large group of my colleagues rushed up to me.

"Hey Jay, where've you been? We didn't see you outside!"

"I was stuck in an elevator and these guys rescued me. Can you get a picture of us?"

My liberators with all their gear looked huge next to me in my gym shorts. I couldn't help thinking, everything is bigger in Texas—even the firemen!

Even being stuck in a smoke-filled elevator couldn't dampen my enthusiasm for exercise. I was right back at it the next day. A good workout gets you out of the office, burns off stress and calories, and helps you maintain a clear head—especially when you need it most!

Find the exercise field trip that works for you!

Field Trip Challenge: Try a new machine, class, or a type of fitness training!

FIELD TRIP POSSIBILITIES

Strength Training: Lift weights, burn calories, and tone your body.

Aerobic Exercise: Walk, run, bike—do something for your lungs and heart every day.

Join a team sport league: Combine aerobic activity with fun, social interactions.

Call-To-Action Plan:

1. Figure out where a workout fits best into your day.
2. Find a gym and sign up!
3. Pack a gym bag with the right gear.
4. Set intentions: how many times a week will you go?
5. Find exercises you like and will commit to.

Take a class: Do Zumba, spin, step, Jazzercise, bootcamp, yoga, dance, water aerobics—the possibilities are endless!

Swim: Laps are low impact and so good for you at any age.

Boxing/Kickboxing: High-impact exercise builds strength and endurance.

Rowing: Combine strength and cardio workouts on the water or in the gym.

Rock climbing: Strengthens your mental focus along with your muscles.

15

Gruetzi

I hit the field-trip jackpot when my company asked me to travel overseas. Taking all-expense-paid trips across the pond seemed like a great deal!

For my first trip, I flew overnight from Boston to Zurich, Switzerland—a new experience in itself. Zurich's airport seemed to be a transfer station to the entire world—I saw people from African countries dressed in colorful garb, Indian women in saris, and other travelers from every possible culture. On the way to customs and baggage claim, I ate the best soft pretzel I'd ever had then topped it off with beautiful French macaroons, which hadn't yet made their way to the United States. The field trip was already awesome—and I hadn't even left the airport!

Even though my meeting was in Lake Lucerne—about an hour away by train—I had planned to explore Zurich. I found my hotel, took a power nap to beat back the jet lag, and headed out to shop on Bahnhofstrasse, which basically means, "the street that leads to the train station." By the time I departed Zurich, I felt like a local since I already knew where to catch the train, which, by the way, counted as another cool field trip. Swiss trains were everything I'd heard—on time, clean, and comfortable.

With only one evening to explore Lake Lucerne, I hurried over to Old Town and walked across Chapel Bridge, a covered, wooden footbridge constructed in 1333.

Strolling along the river Reuss, I took in everything: the surrounding mountains, the medieval architecture, and the pushcarts selling baked goods I had never seen and simply had to try.

"Gruetzi," people would say when I stopped to look at something.

"Greet-zee," I'd reply, trying my best to imitate the Swiss German "hello."

That was the extent of my being able to communicate in any of Switzerland's four national languages—German, French, Italian, and Romansh. Though I did take a year of German in high school, I cheated off my older sister and learned very little. Boy, did I regret that decision on this trip—and future ones! Thankfully, most people I encountered also spoke English, but I made every effort to say "gruetzi" whenever I could. I loved the sound of it and the way it made me feel "in the know."

My exploration of European culture continued the next morning. I was speaking at an event with franchise owners from all over the continent, but by 9:00 a.m., the room was only half full. The German, Austrian, and Swiss contingencies, who had arrived early, repeatedly checked their watches and seemed annoyed.

"Should we start the meeting?" I asked a corporate team member.

"No. We'll wait until the rest of the participants get here."

Around 9:10 a.m. the groups from Spain and Italy finally showed up. But instead of grabbing a coffee and settling into their seats, they chatted at the breakfast buffet outside the meeting room. The first group, now visibly upset, became vocal.

"Excuse me. The schedule said this meeting would start at nine. It's 9:20. Perhaps you could alert the others the meeting will start now?"

The corporate team whisked the latecomers into the room.

That small episode gave me a glimpse into differences I'd later experience when I visited our constituents' countries. German-speaking cultures valued punctuality. Spain and Italy didn't, yet were among the company's best producers. I realized neither approach was right or wrong—just different. But handling the differences at a meeting for them all was definitely tricky!

When we finally started, I opened with, "If you speak three languages, you're trilingual. If you speak two languages, you're bilingual. And if you speak one language, you're American."

They laughed and the tension evaporated.

The cultural exchange continued over lunch, when a guy from the watch-checker contingent asked, "Why do Americans greet someone by saying, 'How are you?' In my experience, the person who asks never waits for a reply. They don't really want to know how you are actually doing."

He had a point. First words are important, and I didn't want mine to be empty, so I stopped greeting strangers with "How are you?" Now I just say "Hello"—unless I'm in Switzerland. Then I say, "Gruetzi!"

You don't need a job that requires overseas travel to explore other cultures—there are endless opportunities right here at home. Just step out of your known world and seek out a new one!

FIELD TRIP:

Explore a new culture!

Field Trip Challenge: Turn an entire day into a foreign-country field trip! Choose a country, do an activity, then enjoy a meal from that region.

SUGGESTIONS FOR EXPLORING OTHER CULTURES:

Call-To-Action Plan:
1. Choose a culture.
2. Plan a related activity.
3. Invite friends or family!
4. Do a post field-trip review.

Visit an ethnic museum: These museums focus on particular ethnic groups. For example, in Watertown, Massachusetts, the Armenian Museum of America has art and artifacts that reveal the history and culture of the Armenian people, many of whom settled in Watertown.

Learn a new language: Online tools make this easier than ever! You can also use the platform Meetup to find conversation groups near you.

Attend a cultural festival/event: Towns across America celebrate their ethnic heritage in all kinds of ways. Check your local listings for events.

Attend a concert: Enjoy exploring different instruments, rhythms, melodies, and stories in another culture's music.

See a foreign film: Trust me, after a minute, you won't even notice the subtitles! But you will get a glimpse into daily life, customs, and language of another culture.

Check out a different culture's art: Explore a different wing of your favorite art museum or seek out exhibits related to a culture you want to experience.

16

Taste Bud Bonanza

For me, food is a field trip. The pretzel and macaroons at the Zurich airport reminded me that mini
field trips can be as memorable as the grand ones!
After a different Switzerland trip, I drove over the
Italian Alps to Milan, Italy, with our Italia group. Milan
seemed chaotic—drivers appeared to ignore traffic laws
and the traffic flow confused me. But the city also gave
an energic vibe with fashionably dressed pedestrians
hurrying along the sidewalks. Everyone seemed to be
chasing a dream.

I gratefully accepted when my colleagues offered to act
as my guides. They took me to their favorite restaurants
and even invited me to their homes for dinner. I loved having an insider's view into the local culture and learning
about Milanese passions—high fashion, Formula One
racing, and Italian football (a.k.a. soccer).

Those meals and interactions were wonderful, but my
most memorable experience happened at a street-side
café. I asked the waiter if they had orange juice.

"Si," he said and returned with a purple-reddish concoction that looked like something from Mars. I had been
in great restaurants and tried new foods all my life but
had never come across anything like this.

"What's this?" I asked.

"Succo d'arancia—orange juice," the server replied.

"This is orange juice?" I asked my colleague, a Canadian who lived in Italy.

He nodded.

"But orange juice is orange," I said. "This is certainly not orange."

"It's juice from a blood orange, a variety grown in the Mediterranean."

Even more strange than the color was the idea that people in other parts of the world experienced orange juice in an entirely different way. No wonder cross-cultural communication can be so difficult!

"Try it," my colleague urged. "It's good."

I took a sip. "Wow! That's delicious!" I downed that first glass and ordered a second and third.

During the rest of my stay, I stopped at produce stands to buy the actual fruit, which looked like regular oranges with a reddish tinge on the outside but were dark purplish-red inside. They tasted like a deeply flavorful orange infused with tart cherries. I simply had to take some home.

On other trips to Europe, I'd try new foods as a matter of course: herring in Sweden, caviar in Turkey, saffron and Iberian ham in Spain. Each taste took me on a field trip that deepened my appreciation for those cultures and gave me the thrill of new discoveries.

Travel is a multi-dimensional field trip with endless opportunities for mini excursions. Don't miss them—even a small taste of something new is an easy way to take a field trip every day!

FIELD TRIP:

Try a new cuisine!

Field Trip Challenge: Don't just eat like a native—cook like one! Research a menu, gather foods and spices from ethnic markets, and create an eating adventure for your friends or family.

Call-To-Action Plan:

1. Find a restaurant that serves food you've never tried.

2. Make a reservation!

3. Invite friends.

4. Do a post field-trip review.

SUGGESTIONS FOR FOOD FIELD TRIPS:

Brazilian: Although I don't eat meat often, I'll always order picanha, a barbecued meat carved right in front of you. It just melts in your mouth. Fried foods don't usually tempt me, but when I hit a Brazilian bakery, I have to have pao de queijo, light and fluffy cheese bread or rolls and bolinho de bacalhau, delicious little fried cod balls. They're a tasty part of Brazil's heritage since salted cod has its roots in Portuguese culture.

Chinese: There's a huge difference between Chinese food and the variety made for the American palate. Try something new, like a quality hotpot or steamed vermicelli rolls. If you haven't tasted a classic dish like Peking duck, make that a field-trip must. Keep exploring! Find a superstar dim sum experience like Yang Sing in San Francisco and sample a huge variety of dumplings. Yum!

East African: Ethiopian and Kenyan dishes come with amazing flavors and spices. I usually go for sukuma wiki (sautéed greens) and the vegetable stews eaten with chapati (flatbread). If you want variety, try the anjero platter with multiple dishes.

French: Until I met Helen, I referred to French cooking as my first love because the sophistication of French dining seemed really cool, and I loved the complex sauces and presentations.

But now I prefer the more basic peasant dishes that typify French cuisine: escargot (snails roasted in garlic and butter), salade nicoise (the salad of all salads made with tuna, hard boiled eggs, olives, and green beans), and cassoulet, a classic stew made with white beans and duck. I finish up with my all-time favorite dessert: apple tarte tatin, an upside-down apple pie cooked in a skillet. It's to die for!

Indian: One of my favorite ways to enjoy Indian food is the Thali lunch. Its several small courses let you sample the cuisine's many flavors and exquisite sauces (cilantro chutney!). If I'm ordering off the menu, I start with malai kofta (veggie meatballs with a thick sauce) and naan (perhaps the best bread anywhere). From there, I'll try whatever suits my mood.

Italian: Italian food is regional. In Northern Italy, I think of sophisticated cuisine, like white or black truffles on pasta or fish (amazing flavor!) or creamy risotto dishes. If I go to Bologna, I have to get Pasta Bolognese, the city's famous, hearty meat sauce. The Adriatic coast has tasty seafood dishes cooked in Mediterranean flavors, and in Southern Italy, I gravitate toward everything with the tangy red sauce.

Japanese: Great sushi chefs give you a mind-numbing variety of tastes with Maki rolls, flavorful combinations of fish, vegetables, and sushi rice wrapped in seaweed. For that reason, I love dining at Japanese restaurants with multiple people so we can let our taste buds go wild. The sushi chef at our local restaurant is so genius, I never order off the menu—I let him decide what to serve me. But if you're new to Japanese food, try the popular bento box, a variety-pack lunch consisting of meat or fish, rice, and veggies.

Mexican: I admit it—I'm in a love affair with guacamole! It's one of the purest dishes in the world because it's so easy to make, so flavorful, and so good for you. If table-side guac is on the menu, I'm ordering it. Let my entrée worry about itself later on.

Portuguese: On my first trip to Portugal, I was blown away by grilled sardines, those tiny fish I had only previously seen in cans. Now I always seek them out at Portuguese restaurants along with polvo a la lagareiro (octopus roasted with olive oil). Sardines and octopus not your thing? Pair caldo verde, a soup made with cabbage rarely found outside of Portugal, with bifanas, a marinated pork sandwich. For dessert, try broa, a delectable egg custard pastry I simply can't resist. In fact, whenever I'm in western Massachusetts, I try to stop at the Ludlow Central Bakery to pick up broa and Portuguese corn bread.

Spanish: Tapas isn't a food but a meal made up of appetizers or small plates, and it's a great way to enjoy many different tastes. For a hearty entrée, try paella, a traditional Spanish dish, made from a crispy base (socarrat), saffron-seasoned rice, and incredible seafood—although variations use other proteins. If meat and cheese plates are an option, taste the Iberian ham.

Thai: At my local Thai restaurant, the waiters bring me the same thing every time— shrimp shumai, shrimp pad Thai with extra lime and extra chopped peanuts, and prik king curry with salmon. If I come in with multiple people, they know I'll want chicken satay, coconut pancakes, and multiple orders of pad Thai.

Turkish: When I first traveled to Turkey, I wanted caviar from the Caspian Sea, but my colleague wanted to take me for testi kebab, casseroles cooked in sealed pottery. The service made this dish an experience—what a show! In Turkish restaurants, I have what I fondly call "the bread series": pide (boat-shaped bread stuffed and heated in a stone oven), durum (kabobs in a wrap), lahmacum (a pizza-like wrap with the best of Turkish flavors), simit (bagels encrusted with sesame seeds), and gozleme (a flatbread stuffed with lamb or spinach and feta). I also recommend balik ekmek, a famous grilled sandwich common in both street carts and restaurants, and manto, fabulous dumplings stuffed with lamb and beef. If you still have room, don't miss the baklava, a syrup-covered, crispy pastry layered with pistachios.

Vietnamese: The first time I experienced Vietnamese cooking, it tasted so light and healthy, I felt great after eating it! Fresh herbs and vegetables make this cuisine incredibly flavorful. Pho (noodle soup flavored with ginger and coriander) is a must. I love goi cuon (translucent spring rolls with greens and coriander) as an appetizer and cha ca (white fish with rice noodles).

17

Downsized

Some work experiences definitely aren't field trips, but if you can ride out the emotional rollercoaster, you just might find ways to pack more fun into your life. Several years ago, I was downsized after eighteen years in the company and twenty-eight in the profession. If you're one of the twenty-five percent who have lost an average of four jobs during their lifetime, then you know the amazing number of emotions you can experience. My rollercoaster looked like this:

Initial exhilaration: FREEDOM! Yeah, I don't have to come in tomorrow!

Reality check: Yikes, I have to report this new situation to Helen. I gave eighteen years—that should be enough—but we still have two daughters in college and a son not far behind.

Disappointment: Where was the loyalty? Where was the golden watch guaranteed to the Silent Generation and the early Baby Boomers?

Self-blame: I had known this was coming, but I hadn't made a plan—and I should have.

Relief: I no longer had the stress of leading a real estate company in the worst market the country had ever seen.

Self-Doubt: How do I find a new identity at fifty-two? Will people within the business look at me differently and think, *that poor guy lost his job?* Will Helen look at me differently and think, *well, he's no longer a big success story?*

I whipped through highs and lows—and that was just the first day.

I needed to figure out the answer to my biggest question: "Where to next?" But first, I had to get myself back to the feel-good zone.

The day after getting the axe, I took phone calls and answered texts and emails from colleagues who wanted to give me their best wishes. I told everyone I now had a new opportunity to take my life back.

On day two, I started accepting invitations for "lunch closure." I wasn't sure if the closure was for me or my colleagues, but either way it provided some fun field trips. Then it was time to ramp up the nature walks, think about the past and the future, and reconnect with my passion.

I knew I no longer wanted a corporate career. Even though I'd held an executive-level position, I still worked for "The Man," and that required me to report. Having a fixed schedule can be good, but it also makes finding work-life balance harder. I wanted to enjoy life by working hard and taking care of my body, mind, and soul. As I saw it, I had three choices:

1. Continue to work for The Man.
2. Start my own company.
3. Take a year off and figure out what to do with the rest of my life.

The opportunity to control my own destiny, work when and where I wanted to, and take any field trip I desired was too great to pass up. I chose door number two and became an entrepreneur. My company, my rules.

Now if I want to take the morning off for a bike ride, I do it. If there's great hiking weather on a Wednesday, I go hiking and work Saturday instead. If I want to see my son play baseball, I make calls while driving to and from the game. My new life has exactly the right balance: work that feels like a field trip and actual field trips! It's really possible, yet so many people think it isn't.

A few years after I started my own company, I was at a dinner party where all the attendees were highly successful people in their prime earning years. Achievement oozed out of everyone's pores as they told each other how impressive they were. (I bet you've seen this show before.) Since I was an outsider, I just listened.

When the testosterone levels came down and someone noticed I was the only person at the table who didn't participate, they turned to me and asked, "What about you, Jay?"

"What about me?"

"What do you do?"

I've never liked that question. Or the "Where do you live?" question. Who said life has to be a scorecard about how much money you make, how big your house is, or what rung of the ladder you're on?

If I was going to play this game, I was going to open up a whole new conversation those people had never thought about: How much fun do you have in your life? How much love do you give and get back?

"I go on a lot of field trips," I said.

The puzzled looks were fantastic. "Field Trips? You mean you chaperone school trips?"

"Well, yes, I've been a chaperone, but my daughters have graduated from college and my son only has a year to go, so now I'm the one who goes on field trips. It's a great gig if you can get it!" I explained recent adventures: whitewater rafting, hiking forty-eight mountains, and finding the best pizza across the country.

The other guests talked about their fantastic vacations, but I brought them back to reality. "Yeah, vacations are great—I highly recommend them—but there should be more to the rest of the year. Every day is a potential field trip!"

Getting downsized definitely wasn't my idea of fun, but it did teach me something: I didn't want that gold watch. I wanted time—time to enjoy the things I value most.

Try a class on becoming an entrepreneur and explore new ways to think about work. It's a field trip that can expand your beliefs about what's possible.

FIELD TRIP:

Take a class on entrepreneurship!

Field Trip Challenge: Start a side gig doing something you love!

SUGGESTED ONLINE COURSES:

Babson Online: Financial Analysis for Decision-Making

Berklee Online: Creativity and Entrepreneurship

Columbia University: Financial Engineering and Risk Management

Harvard Business School online: Entrepreneurship Essentials

MIT Launch: Becoming an Entrepreneur

Call-To-Action Plan:

1. Research online courses on starting your own business. If that doesn't interest you, find a course that will help you grow in your chosen career or launch a new one.
2. Sign up!
3. Do a post field-trip review.

MIT OpenCourseWare: Entrepreneurial Finance

Ohio State University: Branding, Content, and Social Media

Udemy: The Essential Guide to Entrepreneurship by Guy Kawasaki

University of Leeds: Effective Fundraising and Leadership in Arts and Culture

University of Maryland: Corporate Entrepreneurship: Innovating Within Corporations Specialization

PART 3

Building Field Trips Into Family Life

Family expands your field-trip opportunities exponentially—even if you experience hardship. My parents separated when I was young, leaving my mom to start from zero with five kids. Money was so tight we had to ration our food. We felt lucky if we got a new pair of sneakers every now and then. Still, Mom did a great job raising my siblings and me.

We learned teamwork at home because if we didn't help, we wouldn't survive. We forged strong relationships that still keep us connected as adults. We continue to be each other's support network as well as field-trip companions.

Yet every now and then Mom gets sentimental. "I wish I could've given you all more."

I just look at her. "Are you for real? I wouldn't trade one part of how I grew up! You showed us how to survive, love, and overcome a tough situation. How much cooler and inspiring did you want to be?"

Family naturally leads to mini field trips and major, full-scale adventures exploring worlds you never knew existed. And by "family," I don't just mean blood relatives or marital connections; "family" refers to anyone you love.

Whoever your family is, cherish the every-day, field-trip fun that comes with tackling life as part of a team—it's everywhere, and it's fantastic!

18

Helen

If you're lucky, a single event will lead to a lifetime of field trips.

I met Helen at a meeting on the eighty-seventh floor of the World Trade Center Tower One. We worked for the same company—she in the Manhattan office, me in Connecticut.

Weeks later at a corporate event, we agreed to gather with colleagues afterward, but everyone else bailed, leaving just the two of us. I asked if she wanted to grab a bite on the concourse downstairs. She said yes.

We had a fun night and when it was over, we both headed to the subway station. I thought it was one way, but Helen insisted it was another.

"You willing to bet on that?" I asked.

"Sure," Helen said.

"Okay. Whoever is wrong has to buy the other dinner."

"Deal!"

Helen was right, but I felt like a winner because I got to take her out.

We dined at the famous Smith & Wollensky steak house, where I discovered she liked New York baseball, too. She rooted for both the Yankees and the Mets. I didn't care either way—she had me at baseball.

When our date ended, I left her at Grand Central Station. I instinctively looked back and saw she was looking back at me. So, I invited her to see the Yankees play the Red Sox. The Yankees lost by one run but sitting next to Helen made that loss less painful.

Our fourth date, to see the Mets at Shea Stadium, should have given Helen fair warning about life with Jay. I didn't buy tickets in advance because there should have been plenty, but the game was sold out when we arrived at the park. (The Mets had a winning season that year, which eventually led to a World Series win over the Red Sox.)

No problem—I went to Plan B: buy tickets from a scalper.

Once inside the park, we discovered our seats were in a section under renovation—the tickets weren't valid! Undeterred, I found empty seats nearby. When the ticketholders showed up, we moved. Each time we got kicked out was a mini field trip within the stadium. We had such a good time, we decided to keep the date going with dinner and a movie.

I must have gotten better at planning dates because Helen stuck with me. We discovered we shared an excitement for going different places and doing new things. Thirty-four years later, we're still together.

My best life doesn't happen without Helen. I never knew I could love someone so much. When Caitlin was born, I found I had more love in the tank, and even more with Michaela, and still more with Kevin. Family kept expanding my capacity for love and joy.

That one after-work field trip led to a lifetime of others. Helen and I—and our three children—have attended hundreds of baseball and softball games, taken tons of fun outings, and enjoyed just being in each other's company on countless mini field trips.

Finding a life partner may involve luck, but fun doesn't. Whether you're single or married, create some good times with the people you love. Plan a special night out that gets everyone off their screens, out of the house, and into a memorable experience!

Plan a family (or friends) night out!

Field Trip Challenge: Take a family road trip! Plan an overnight or a multiple-day excursion. Get as many family members as you can, but be flexible! If someone can only attend one day or even part of a day, roll with that. Consider trips to national parks, Disney, or other fun, family-friendly locations.

Call-To-Action Plan:

1. Find an outing the whole family would enjoy.

2. Buy tickets and plan the details.

3. Do a post field-trip review.

SUGGESTIONS FOR A FAMILY NIGHT OUT:

Comedy: Who doesn't love to laugh? Go to a comedy club or buy tickets for big-name comedians like Sebastian Maniscalco, Mike Birbiglia, and John Mulaney.

Music Concerts: Take in shows the entire family will enjoy or go to different shows with particular family members. I just saw Brandi Carlile with my daughter, Rob Thomas with Helen, and Bon Iver with a friend.

Live Theater Experiences: Find a show that'll turn your gang into live-theater fans: a play, a musical, a themed ice-skating show—you name it.

National Geographic Live Events: Look for live events that explore behind the scenes stories from the front lines of exploration.

19

The Bus Stop

When you have young kids, it's easy to work field trips into almost anything. The bus stop— the day's first recess—let both me and my kids burn off a little energy before hunkering down at our desks.

Many parents don't take advantage of this easy opportunity for fun. They stand around holding their coffee mugs and chatting. It's like they've forgotten how to play! Forget caffeine—the best way to kick off the day is to rustle up a game and get everyone to join in.

When my kids were young, I'd hustle them out the door ten minutes early and grab some kind of ball. We all loved to play sports, so why not squeeze some in before the bus arrived? If I had the soccer ball, we practiced footwork or played a mini game in our suburban street. (In the city, it can be a more controlled game on the sidewalk.) Or sometimes I'd grab a football to throw around.

The kids (mine and whoever else wanted to join in) scored goals or made catches and practiced their best versions of the touchdown dance.

Once the bus arrived, I'd already taken a mini field trip, activated my endorphins, and walked home with a little more jump in my step.

If I'd understood the power of walking back then, I would've taken a longer route home and fit in two field trips before I left for work. But I had discounted walking as exercise until I was forty and needed surgery. A physician friend warned me about overexertion during the recovery.

"Jay, I know within a week you're gonna want to get back on the basketball court," he said. "But don't do it. Your body needs to heal for a full eight weeks. Walking should be your only exercise."

I walked four miles every day for eight weeks. To give my lungs a workout, I chose a route with rolling hills. When I was finally able to play basketball again, I thought I'd be out of gas after fifteen minutes. But I played for ninety! Daily walks had kept my lungs and legs in great shape.

Life is busy, so your next field trip is a walk in the park—literally! Keep it simple and stay local or plan a walking adventure for everyone!

FIELD TRIP:

Take a walk!

Field Trip Challenge:
Build a walk into your daily routine by taking one every day at the same time for thirty days.

Call-To-Action Plan:

1. Choose a location.
2. Plan a time.
3. Invite someone along.
4. Do a post field-trip review.

SUGGESTED WALKING LOCATIONS:

The City: When I travel to a new city, the first thing I do is take a walk. I want to get to know the city, feel the pulse, see the people, and know I'm in the moment wherever I am.

The Burbs: Enjoy the sidewalks alone or with a friend or family member. One Father's Day, I wanted to walk a marathon (26.2 miles) around my own neighborhood, so my three kids and my wife took turns walking with me.

Walking Trails: There are more great trails than ever before. Check out the ones near you.

Hiking Trails: See Chapter 31.

State Parks: Make it a goal to walk all the state parks in your region.

Local Parks: Plan a walk with a friend in one of the many local parks in your area.

National Parks: Explore the many walking paths in the sixty-three national parks.

National Forests: Find great walks in any of the 154 national forests.

The Beach: If you don't live near one, it's worth taking a drive to walk on the beach.

The Track: Not my favorite, but some people love walking in a big circle.

The Mall: Many malls open early to allow walkers to get their exercise.

20

The Beach

Being part of a family often means compromising on field trips. My lovely bride grew up near the ocean and loves the beach, while I prefer the mountains. But that's okay, because I can have fun anywhere—except when I wind up in the ER!

My family once took a vacation to St. John in the Virgin Islands. Helen had been looking forward to our trip because she finds the beach a sanctuary from life's hectic pace and New England's harsh winters. Nothing says relaxation like the smell of saltwater, the whoosh of the waves, and sand between her toes.

After we arrived, I thought I'd endear myself to my wife by entertaining the kids around the resort while she relaxed on the beach. We'd join her a few hours later.

Right on schedule, the kids and I made our way to the ocean. I picked up a newspaper as we passed the mini front desk at the edge of the sand. Looking down at the headlines, I walked hard into a hefty metal sign.

I've played a lot of contact sports, so bumping into something wasn't a big deal. I tried to shake it off, but when the kids started screaming and blood gushed like Old Faithful into my eyes and mouth, I realized I'd split open my forehead. Who knew so much blood comes out of a forehead?!

Someone gave me a towel to press against the wound and we proceeded to look for Helen. "We're here," I started to say, but the kids talked over me.

"Daddy ran into a sign!"

"He's bleeding everywhere!"

Helen jumped up. "Oh my gosh, Jay! What happened?"

"I bumped into a sign."

Some resort staff came over and told me to sit down, which was a good thing, because I had started to get really light-headed. Minutes later, Helen took me to the hospital, where I learned my "minor" cut required stitches.

So much for endearing myself to her! Not only didn't she get her day at the beach, I was banned from water sports for the rest of our vacation.

I wish I could say that was one unlucky incident, but on another beach vacation, I sliced open my toes walking through a screen door between our hotel room and patio. That ended all my water activities that time as well.

Though I might be safer in the mountains, I hold no ill will towards beach vacations! When I manage to stay out of the ER, I still love being on the water and letting Helen bask in the sun's warm glow.

Every state in the U.S. has either a coast, a lake over fifty square miles, or a large river. Round up your clan and head to the water where you'll find incredible opportunities for family fun!

FIELD TRIP:

Gather your crew and find a beach/water adventure near you!

Field Trip Challenge: Make it a goal to visit every beach in your state!

SUGGESTED ACTIVITIES FOR BEACH FIELD TRIPS:

Call-To-Action Plan:

1. Plan a day at the beach.
2. Gather the appropriate gear—don't forget sunscreen!
3. Round up the family and have fun in the sun.
4. Do a post field-trip review.

Surf

Swimming

Boating

Kayaking

Canoeing

Paddle boarding

Wakeboarding

Jet skiing

Water skiing

Fishing

Sailing

Surfing

Scuba diving

Snorkeling

Tubing

Cruises

White-water rafting (rivers)

Parasailing (lakes and oceans)

Whale watching (ocean)

Deep-sea fishing (ocean)

Turf

Picnics

Reading

Naps

Wildlife viewing

Hiking

Biking

Photography

Sunbathing

Kite flying

People watching

Games (Cam Jam, corn hole, frisbee)

Sports

Birding

Sandcastles

21

School Trips

It's one thing to take your own kids on a field trip—it's another to take a group of school kids on one. Don't miss it!

The first time my daughter asked if I would volunteer to chaperone her school trip, I jumped at the chance to travel down memory lane to the great field trips of my youth. But the school had too many volunteers; I lost my bid to hop a yellow school bus and sing "99 Bottles of Beer on the Wall."

Lucky for me, I had many other opportunities over the years—I probably even made a name for myself as "The Chaperone." But the fifth-grade trip to the Mashantucket Pequot Museum in Connecticut really stands out.

Since I was the only male chaperone, the quick-witted teacher put all the challenging boys under my watch. "Keep a close eye on them!"

Wow—the pressure! All parents have nightmares about losing their child at a busy park, city, or mall. Now I had to worry about rambunctious boys slipping away in a museum complex.

I soon found the boys in my group definitely had their own ideas about how the field trip would go down. When the girls went right, they went left. If the girls showed interest in an exhibit, the boys pranked them. They continued nonstop for the first sixty minutes. My patience wore thin.

I wracked my brain for a system to keep everyone together. Out of nowhere, a line of preschoolers appeared, holding onto a rope.

That's weird, I thought. *Why would their teachers have them hold onto something that looks like a leash?* I put two and two together and came up with an idea so crazy it just might work.

I gathered my fifth graders in a huddle. "Look kids, the school and your parents bestowed their faith in my ability to return each of you to the bus at the end of the day. From the bottom of my heart, I really want to be the cool Dad, but I've reached the proverbial end of the line. I'm imposing a new rule. If even one person strays from the group, everyone will have to hold hands for the rest of the day."

It worked!

As we filed onto the bus to ride back to school, the teacher approached me. "How was your group, Mr. Hummer?"

"Perfect angels," I replied. "Perfect angels."

Chaperoning school trips checks all the boxes for a great field trip: you step out of your routine, learn something new, and remind yourself what it's like to be a kid.

Go ahead and volunteer!

FIELD TRIP:

Chaperone a school trip!

Field Trip Challenge:
Chaperone your own field trips.

Invite a group of your child's friends to do something fun! If you're a grandparent, a big brother, big sister, or trusted relative, you, too, can offer to chaperone a field trip for a child you love and their friends.

Call-To-Action Plan:

1. Chaperone next time there's a school field trip.

2. Arrange to take the day off from work.

3. Research how to be a fun chaperone.

4. Enjoy spending the day with your child and their classmates!

5. Do a post field-trip review.

If you don't have children in your life, find a local nonprofit that could use your chaperone support.

22

Band Trip

No matter how many field trips I take, there is always more fun to be had by jumping into new experiences. But even I had misgivings about chaperoning my oldest daughter's freshman-year band trip to Maryland. It was one thing to give up control of my destiny for a one-hour bus ride, but an eight-hour trip presented new complications.

What if I needed to stretch my legs? Would the bus driver see me in his little mirror and yell, "Hey, you with the funny shirt, sit down!" Would there be bathroom breaks? Or were there bathrooms on the bus and if so, would they smell? The entire month before the trip, I dreaded being cooped up for hours in a noisy, smelly, uncomfortable bus.

On the day of reckoning, I drove into the school parking lot and what to my wondering eyes appeared? No miniature sleigh with eight tiny reindeer, but something even more magical—two glistening coach buses!

As the band and choir gathered for instructions, I scoped out the buses and chose Bob's. Bob suggested I sit up front, so we could chat while he drove. I settled into the first row, and looked through the big, beautiful window. Perfect! Just me, Bob, the road ahead, and about fifty excited band members behind us.

But when I tuned into the kids, I was immersed in a different culture. I stopped playing in the band after seventh grade, so my experience with "Band Geeks" (as the trip members called themselves) was limited. What I found was a more fun, witty, and carefree group than the stereotyped groups of my past.

As I watched my daughter interact with her fellow musicians, I realized she cherished band even more than softball, a sport she worked hard at. It wasn't just that she liked playing her instrument and understood music's language; she had found her people in the peer-pressure incubator known as high school.

The dreaded eight-hour bus trip turned out to be surprisingly interesting—and enjoyable. It got even more fun when we finally arrived at the hotel and Bob switched gears from bus driver to field-trip organizer. A guitarist himself, he arranged for a meeting room and told the kids to spread the word about a jam session. Within thirty minutes, he and more than half the band members gathered for some impromptu musical play. Everyone took turns suggesting tunes and improvising. The choir kids sang, danced, or just listened. All those kids so loved music, I couldn't help loving it, too.

After the next day's competition, we boarded the bus for a side trip to Washington, D.C.

"Hey, you know the city," Bob said. "Want to play tour guide?"

Tour guide! The ruler of the bus, the only one with a mic, the only one allowed to stand. I could make jokes or even dance down the aisle as I offered a running commentary on the national monuments and museums we passed. What a blast!

(Definitely finagle your way into the tour-guide role if you can. It's a mini field trip within a field trip!)

Every adventure has taught me something new, and the band outing was no exception. I understood my daughter better and learned that I'm not only a huge fan of guitar-playing bus drivers, jam sessions, and the band's cool culture, I also love being a tour guide!

You won't need to hop a bus for your next field trip—stay local and find a youth music event near you. Let eager, young performers inspire you with their infectious form of play—music!

FIELD TRIP:

Attend a youth music event!

Field Trip Challenge: Dust off your own instrument and start playing again. Or, if you've always wanted to play one, sign up for lessons!

SUGGESTIONS FOR YOUTH MUSIC EVENTS:

School Band Concerts: Most schools have concerts during the fall, winter, and spring. That adds up to three built-in field trips per school year.

School Choir Concerts: Many schools have multiple choir groups—mixed choirs, women's choirs, acapella, and more.

Call-To-Action Plan:

1. Check the websites of local middle schools, high schools, and colleges for music event schedules.

2. Invite friends and neighbors to come along!

3. Purchase tickets.

4. Enjoy an inexpensive, high-quality music event!

5. Do a post field-trip review.

School Orchestra Concerts: You could enjoy this experience so much you might decide to visit the local symphony. Maybe you'll even expand to the opera!

School Plays and Musicals: School theater departments have an amazing amount of talent on display in their theater productions and musicals. Most shows have multiple performances. My lovely bride and I still attend the shows at our high school even though our children have graduated.

Parades: Who doesn't love a parade? Pencil in Memorial Day and Fourth of July as parade field trips. Many communities have spirit days or weekends where parades happen. You might get so fired up you'll want to attend the Macy's Thanksgiving Day Parade in New York City or the Rose Bowl Parade in Pasadena, California.

23

Bad Day of Baseball

Field-trip opportunities multiply with kids. Besides those associated with school—bus stops, concerts, and trips—countless others stem from extra-curricular activities.

In the Hummer house, baseball is a birthright. I coached my two daughters in softball and my son in baseball. With more than eighty games a year plus practices, off-season training sessions, and backyard catches and batting practice, I had a field trip just about every day for fifteen years.

Even more than the physical workouts, I loved the mental challenges of coaching. It's not easy to help young people believe they can develop the specialized abilities necessary to succeed in a particular sport. Catching, hitting, throwing, and base-running are all difficult but learnable skills, yet kids don't always see it that way. They struggle with frustration if they can't easily make plays or win games.

My own children felt disheartened by bad losses or poor performances. One day, my son was down on himself after back-to-back losses in a double header. He'd gone up to the plate five times and made five outs.

"Buddy," I said, as we ate pizza afterward, "would you agree that a bad day of baseball is better than a good day of school?"

He looked up at me and smiled. "Yes, so it is."

If kids play sports, it's inevitable they'll have days when they don't personally perform well. Too many bad-baseball days can lead to giving up, which is why I always felt terrible when I couldn't help a child find success. That was the hardest part of coaching.

After one game, I expressed frustration to my friend, a division-one college hockey coach who had a daughter on my team. "No matter what I do, I can't get this one player to succeed at the plate."

"Do you think she wants to succeed?" he asked.

"Yes."

"Is she working hard to succeed?"

"Yes."

I realized it was up to me to help her and dug deeper into the problem. Her hitting mechanics (stance, load, timing, and swing) were great. She was just missing the ball. Did she need glasses? I asked her parents about her eyesight. They had it checked, and sure enough, she did. Once that young lady could see the ball better, she found success that season and enjoyed the game for a couple more years. It was an eye opener for both of us.

I didn't want to lose a kid because I failed them as a coach, so I continually asked myself, what's the difference between the players who quit and those who persist long enough to make their school teams?

Long before he became a Super Bowl hero, Julian Edelman, the great wide receiver for the New England Patriots, made a commercial with me and my kids when he was still an NFL rookie. Talking about youth sports during a break, he said, "The others didn't work as hard as me. I never let anyone outwork me."

His story certainly backed it up. He didn't just walk into a starting lineup position like many top draft picks. He played quarterback at Kent State—not Alabama, Oklahoma, or one of the big college football factories. To land a spot in the NFL, he had to work hard to turn himself into a wide receiver. Eventually, he helped create one of the greatest football dynasties.

What, I wondered, inspired him to work that hard, and how could I light the same kind of fire under my own players? I couldn't find an answer in any of the many coaching books I poured through, so the question still dogged me when I took on a new challenge: coaching ten-year-old softball players who didn't make the town's top two teams.

Like so many of the girls on that team, Katy was already motivated to put in a lot of effort during practice. She ran hard and was fast, a perfect candidate to patrol the outfield. There was only one problem: she couldn't catch a fly ball.

I asked Katy and her dad to stay after practice one day and had him stand beside me while I took her through a number of basic outfield drills. She worked really hard and did catch a few fly balls, but she still needed a lot more practice. When we finished, I gave her and her dad an assignment that required a big commitment: go through the drills and then take 100 fly balls every day.

As the season progressed, the drills paid off—she tracked down many fly balls that could have been base hits. I can't begin to describe how proud I was of her as she evolved into a real asset for the team.

But hard work and improved mechanics are only part of her story. The truth is, Katy couldn't have succeeded on her own. She needed someone to hit those fly balls to her, and luckily her dad shared a love for softball and wanted to support her. Every night they had a meaningful—and fun—field trip as they worked on those drills together.

Love, fun, and joy are all powerful drivers that turn work into play and lead to success. Julian Edelman was a star player because he worked hard at football, but he had to love football to work so hard at it.

The whole point of field trips is to explore what's out there, find things we love—and keep doing them! I coached because I loved sports, spending time with my kids, and tackling leadership challenges. When your glory days are behind you, keep your passion alive by teaching kids something you're good at. Coaching sports teams or arts activities in your town—or wherever volunteers are needed—provides an endless source of gratifying field trips.

Until you're ready to make that leap, find a local or school team to support, grab a spot on the bleachers, and cheer on the young athletes! You just might help tomorrow's leaders gain confidence while they learn from good and bad days of baseball.

FIELD TRIP:

Go to a youth, high school, or college game!

Field Trip Challenge:
Follow a team for a
whole season!

SUGGESTIONS FOR YOUTH SPORTS FIELD TRIPS:

Little League Baseball & Softball: There are over 180,000 Little League teams throughout the country and the world: most leagues range from tee ball, farm league, instructional, minors, and the major leagues (ages ten to twelve).

Call-To-Action Plan:
1. Find a local game in a sport you enjoy.
2. Invite a buddy to watch with you.
3. Cheer on the home team!
4. Do a post field-trip review.

The Little League World Series is a such big—and exclusive—deal, you can watch the games on national television. Players, coaches, and parents yearn to get to Williamsport, Pennsylvania for a shot at the title.

Give yourself the field trip of following your local Little League team for an entire season. See the kids as they grow and watch the stars shine. Then follow the all-star tournaments for kids ages nine through twelve. Root them on! Whoever wins, you can cheer for them at the state tournament.

Cal Ripken Baseball: Yes, the Iron Man himself started Cal Ripken Baseball Leagues—which have their own tournaments—throughout the country. If you live in Maryland or South Carolina, you can watch teams from across the U.S.

compete at the Cal Ripken Experience Parks.

American Legion Baseball: Legion Baseball starts after the high-school season ends. Follow your team in the regular season, through the district tournament, state tournament, regionals, and even to the American Legion World Series held in Shelby, North Carolina every August.

Babe Ruth Baseball: This also starts following the high-school season. Watch your team play the regular season and the championship series all the way through the All-Star Tournament, and then root for them in the National finals.

Amateur Athletic Union (AAU) Baseball: With AAU baseball, kids from age eight through thirteen can play more games against better competition. The AAU schedule gives younger players the chance to play two doubleheaders each weekend as well as tournaments and season championships.

Showcase Baseball: This is not a sanctioned league. After high-school season ends, ultra-competitive teams try to attract college scouts by playing showcase tournaments every weekend. For players at this level, the draw is simple: to be seen by college scouts.

Fastpitch Softball: The softball governing bodies of the American Softball Association (ASA), the National Softball Association (NSA), and Pony Baseball and Softball host tournaments across the country. The players at these tournaments start at age eight and go all the way to age twenty-three. Go to the ASA, NSA, and PONY websites and find tournaments in your state. These events usually start at 8:00 a.m. and finish as late as 10:00 p.m. Nonstop softball!

MORE SPORTS TEAMS TO ROOT FOR:

Youth leagues in every sport are really popular now. Field hockey, volleyball, lacrosse, and football have games to watch for a day or teams to follow for a season.

High-school girls' or boys' sports teams offer field trips throughout the academic year.

Colleges give you an opportunity to watch talented, committed athletes play at another level. Community College, National Association of Intercollegiate Athletics (NAIA), and National Collegiate Athletic Association (NCAA) have divisions one, two, and three in every sport imaginable.

At my son's college baseball game, I asked a guy if he had a son on the other team. "I don't," he replied. "I live locally and follow the team every year."

That's the spirit!

24

Moosing

My friend Steve was desperate to see a moose, so he invited me and my teenage son to join him and his son on a moosing field trip in New Hampshire. Moose help drive tourism in northern New England. Skiers, summer vacationers, and fall leaf-peepers all hope to glimpse the animal whose silhouette appears on gift-shop merchandise everywhere. Thousands of people who have never seen one—like my brother and other constant visitors to New Hampshire's White Mountains—don't believe they even exist. Yet, if you talk to a local, they'll tell you what a pain these creatures are. Everyone has a story!

Steve, an accomplished photographer, was determined to get pictures, so he insisted we get up before 6:00 a.m. since moose are most active at dawn and dusk. We drove up and down country roads, scouring the woods until dawn turned into day. Then we repeated the ritual at dusk, giving up only when darkness made it impossible to see. For three days, Steve was ready with his camera but found nothing to show for it. I understood his passion but was tired of looking for Bullwinkle.

One morning, we mentioned our failed moose-sighting attempts to the owner of the bed and breakfast where we were staying. She recommended we hire her friend, the self-proclaimed "best mooser of the area."

"I guarantee you'll see a moose," the owner said.

"What do you think?" Steve asked me.

"Well," I replied, "we've already taken the inexpensive field trip by driving around on our own, but it's not getting us anywhere. If you really want to see a moose, a guide might be your best bet."

He hired the area's Best Mooser. When she arranged to pick us up as twilight faded, we learned our first mistake—we hadn't waited for darkness.

"How will we see the moose?" Steve asked.

Pointing at the big spotlights in her truck, she explained, "It's against the law to use lights to hunt animals at night, but it's perfectly legal if you're just looking at them."

"I only intend to shoot them with this," Steve said, showing her his camera. "I just hope I can get a shot before total darkness descends."

With a new spirit of adventure, we slid into the guide's truck and slowly drove along the same roads we'd already traveled. Our sons had a blast shining the spotlights into the woods and, sure enough, those lights revealed three moose staring out at us from among the trees. Steve hopped out of the truck to get a photo even though there was hardly any light. I have no idea if it came out, but it didn't matter—he'd achieved his bucket-list goal!

Nighttime opens up even more opportunities for field-trip fun, so why not switch things up and head out after dark? Even familiar experiences can feel new when the sun goes down!

Explore what happens at night!

Field Trip Challenge: Take a nighttime field trip once every season!

SUGGESTIONS FOR NIGHTTIME FIELD TRIPS:

Catch fireflies: Hustle the little ones into the backyard and let them chase, capture, and marvel at the tiny flying light bulbs.

Call-To-Action Plan:

1. Choose a nighttime adventure.
2. Take a nap!
3. Gather the appropriate gear.
4. Round up the kids or a few friends.
5. Do a post field-trip review.

Moosing: Head to the northern and mountain states, find a guide, and see these magnificent creatures in their natural habitat.

Night hikes or walks: Purchase a good head lamp—it will light your way better than a flashlight—and head out on the trail. If you face it into the trees, you might see wildlife staring back at you! If you prefer a guided night hike, check online to find naturalists who lead moonlit nature walks.

Night skiing: If you love hitting the slopes during the day, find a mountain that offers night skiing. Or pull out that head lamp and try cross-country skiing for a great evening workout.

Night water adventures: Find organizations that lead night swims or dives. If you can get to Puerto Rico, swim in a bioluminescent bay. If you want to stay dry while you enjoy the water, consider a nighttime boating experience.

Owling: Listen for hooting and track down the source. These cool birds are amazing to see.

Stargazing: Wait for a clear dark night and look up! You can locate the constellations and watch for satellites orbiting the earth with the naked eye. See more by connecting with a stargazing group equipped with telescopes. Check online for annual meteor showers and watch the "stars" shoot across the night sky!

Try any favorite activity at night: Places like zoos, museums, corn mazes, etc., usually offer nighttime experiences. Check them out and put a new spin on a familiar outing!

25

Fairway Friends

My childhood zoo field trips obviously made an impression on me; I always relished the chance to see live animals—even when it wasn't a good idea. Once while playing golf at the spectacular Banff Springs Golf Club in Alberta, Canada, I saw an imposing elk a mere ten feet from my ball. Undaunted, I walked right up to the ball and hit it down the fairway. (Okay, maybe it wasn't right down the fairway.)

I should have continued on my way, but I didn't. The elk seemed unfazed by my presence, so I just stood there looking at it. It looked right back at me, apparently as curious as I was. Maybe it likes my outfit, I thought.

I'd heard these animals will charge if they feel threatened. They're also faster than horses, so my golf cart would be useless if I needed a quick getaway. Since I didn't want to test my luck, I put an end to our staring contest after a few seconds.

When my buddy and I hit the fifteenth tee box a few holes later, the course warden stopped by to let us know a grizzly bear was on the sixteenth fairway. My already-poor golf game became totally insignificant—I wanted to see a live grizzly!

I looked everywhere as we played the next hole, but the bear was nowhere in sight. After wrapping up the game, my friend and I decided to look for the bear. We didn't see it.

Later that evening, I ran into a wildlife specialist at the hotel bar. I told her about my elk encounter.

"Be careful," she said. "If an elk puts its ears back, it's preparing to charge."

"Hey, the elk did twitch its ears just as I was heading back to the cart."

"You're lucky. Another second and you might've been pummeled."

She didn't know the half of it! I probably would've survived the elk, but the grizzly? Not so much.

That night—and even to this day—I wondered about my decision to go looking for the bear. What was I thinking? And why did my friend agree to join me? What was he thinking?!

Months later, I asked him.

"I knew you already had a pulled hamstring," he replied, grinning, "so I figured the old adage was true. I didn't have to outrun the bear—I only had to outrun you!"

Seeing wildlife in their natural habitats is always a cool experience, but don't push your luck like I did. Be careful! Wild animals aren't pets—they can cause serious injury and even death. Skip the close selfie, respect the animals' space, and keep everyone safe.

Or better yet, view wildlife in a zoo! My family loves seeing animals from different parts of the world. With 2,400 zoos and 470 other licensed zoological facilities in the U.S., there's bound to be a safe yet spectacular wildlife field trip near you.

FIELD TRIP:

See wildlife at the zoo!

Field Trip Challenge: Find a safari park in the U.S. to safely see wild animals living in their habitats.

Suggestions for zoo field trips: The following list includes zoos my family has visited and others still on our radar.

Call-To-Action Plan:

1. Choose a zoo adventure.
2. Research ticket prices.
3. Plan your transportation.
4. Round up the kids and go!
5. Do a post field-trip review.

NORTHEAST

Massachusetts: Franklin Park Zoo (Boston), Southwick's Zoo (Mendon)

New Jersey: Cape May County Park & Zoo

New York: Bronx Zoo and Central Park Zoo (New York City)

Pennsylvania: ZooAmerica (Hershey), Pittsburgh Zoo & PPG Aquarium (Highland Park), Philadelphia Zoo

Rhode Island: Roger Williams Park Zoo (Providence)

MIDWEST

Illinois: Lincoln Park Zoo (Chicago), Brookfield Zoo (Brookfield)

Indiana: Indianapolis Zoo

Iowa: Blank Park Zoo (Des Moines)

Kansas: Sedgwick County Zoo (Wichita)

Minnesota: Minnesota Zoo (Apple Valley)

Nebraska: Omaha's Henry Doorly Zoo and Aquarium

Ohio: Cincinnati Zoo, Cleveland MetroParks Zoo, Detroit Zoo (Royal Oak), The Wilds Columbus Zoo and Aquarium (Cumberland)

South Dakota: Bear Country USA (Rapid City)

Wisconsin: Milwaukee County Zoo

SOUTHEAST

Alabama: Birmingham Zoo

Arkansas: Little Rock Zoo

Florida: Lion Country Safari, Disney's Animal Kingdom, Busch Gardens (Tampa), Brevard Zoo (Melbourne), Zoo Miami

Georgia: Zoo Atlanta

Kentucky: Louisville Zoo

Louisiana: Audubon Zoo (New Orleans)

Maryland: Maryland Zoo (Baltimore)

Mississippi: Jackson Zoo

Missouri: Saint Louis Zoo

North Carolina: North Carolina Zoo

South Carolina: Greenville Zoo

Tennessee: Memphis Zoo, Nashville Zoo at Grassmere

Virginia: Virginia Zoo (Norfolk)

Washington D.C.: National Zoo

SOUTHWEST

Texas: Houston Zoo, Fort Worth Zoo, Dallas Zoo, San Antonio Zoo

Arizona: Phoenix Zoo, Arizona-Sonora Desert Museum (Tucson), Out of Africa Wildlife Park (Camp Verde)

Oklahoma: Oklahoma City Zoo

WEST

Alaska: Alaska Zoo (Anchorage)

California: San Diego Zoo, The Living Desert Zoo and Gardens (Palm Springs), Oakland Zoo, Los Angeles Zoo, San Francisco Zoo, Safari West (Santa Rosa)

Colorado: Denver Zoo

Hawaii: Honolulu Zoo

Idaho: World Center for Birds of Prey (Boise)

Montana: ZooMontana (Billings)

Oregon: Oregon Zoo (Portland)

Washington: Woodland Park Zoo (Seattle)

Wyoming: Cheyenne Mountain Zoo

TAKE A ONCE-IN-A-LIFETIME WILDLIFE TRIP!

Australia: Kangaroo Island

Borneo: Kinabatangan River

Botswana: Chobe National Park, Okavango Delta

Brazil: The Pantanal

China: Tibetan Plateau

Costa Rica: Corcovado National Park

India: Kanha Tiger Reserve

Kenya: Masai Mara National Reserve

South Africa: Addo Elephant Park, Kruger National Park

Tanzania: Serengeti National Park

Thailand: Kaeng Krachan National Park

Zambia: South Luangwa National Park

26

Sea and Air

Boating field trips give me pause. Don't get me wrong—I love rivers, lakes, and blue ocean water up to my chest. Beyond that, though, things get dicey because the sea is powerful.

Storms? It has the biggest.

Creatures? You bet—the largest!

Predators? Oh yeah—the fiercest.

Unknowns? You guessed it—the most.

That's why I dance lightly around seafaring.

But Helen grew up near the beach and feels comfortable on boats. She and the kids love to cruise the waters around New York City on her father's twenty-three-foot cabin cruiser. I usually decline these outings in favor of land-based activities like biking, hiking, or golf. But one late October day, I said yes to a boating field trip.

The temperature was cool, so we dressed in jeans and jackets to stay warm. My father-in-law took us out on Jamaica Bay, and everything went as planned—until we returned to the dock.

"Hey Jay, can you give me a hand?" he asked.

"Sure! What do you want me to do?"

"As soon as I get closer, grab the line and hop on the dock. After you pull in the boat, wind the rope around the cleat." He pointed to the horn-shaped fitting on the dock.

"No problem. Happy to help!" Line in hand, I jumped my athletic self onto the pier. As I pulled the great ship toward me, the knots that tied the line to the cruiser suddenly came loose. I stumbled backwards and—splash! I fell into the drink.

My daughter—four at the time—started screaming. She thought the sea had swallowed me.

"See, Daddy's fine," Helen soothed Caitlin as I hoisted myself onto the dock. "Jay, are you okay?"

"Yeah, I'm fine."

Then Helen and my father-in-law burst out laughing.

Despite that mishap, I didn't give up on seafaring adventures. I just made sure to choose a safer, warmer spot.

I once tacked on an extra day for a tour of Biscayne National Park during a Florida business trip. Since the park is ninety-five percent water, it makes for a fantastic boating field trip. Luckily, no one else signed up, so the captain let me decide how to spend the next several hours.

She motored over to Jones Lagoon so we could paddle board around its clear, shallow waters. I saw barracudas, small sharks, jellyfish, stingrays, and the most colorful fish you can imagine. And that was just the wildlife under my feet.

The surrounding mangroves housed a bird sanctuary teeming with tropical species. The captain pointed out frigatebirds, anhingas, blue herons, and countless other winged creatures going about their daily activities. Roseate Spoonbills waded along the shoreline, brown pelicans flew overhead, and spotted sandpipers darted along the water's edge.

"I'm good here," I told the captain. "No need to take me anywhere else."

I had the best of two distinct wildlife worlds—sea and air—and didn't know whether to look down or up! Something about their natural beauty and harmony filled me with awe—like the first time I saw a bald eagle in the wild.

I'd only ever seen bald eagles in zoos, but when I heard they're commonly spotted at Umbagog Lake in New Hampshire, I took my family there on a field trip. A guide showed us one of their huge nests, and then we saw the eagle's magnificent seven-foot wingspan as it soared across the lake. What a thrilling moment for a patriotic American and wildlife lover.

If you want to experience spectacular wildlife without getting in over your head, no need to visit Biscayne, get on a boat, or go anywhere near a dock. Just head to an aquarium or a bird sanctuary near you! Both are safe, warm, and dry places to see remarkable creatures from two vastly different worlds.

FIELD TRIP:

Take a trip to the aquarium or a bird sanctuary!

Field Trip Challenge: Two field trips are always better than one, right? Plan one adventure to view sea life and another to see birds.

Suggestions for sea-life field trips:

NORTHEAST

Massachusetts: New England Aquarium (Boston)

New York: New York Aquarium (Brooklyn)

New Jersey: Adventure Aquarium (Camden)

MIDWEST

Illinois: Shedd Aquarium (Chicago)

Ohio: Newport Aquarium (Cincinnati)

SOUTHEAST

Florida: Florida Aquarium (Tampa), Miami Seaquarium (Miami)

Georgia: Georgia Aquarium (Atlanta)

Louisiana: Audubon Aquarium of the Americas (New Orleans)

Maryland: National Aquarium (Baltimore)

South Carolina: Ripley's Aquarium (Myrtle Beach), South Carolina Aquarium (Charleston)

Call-To-Action Plan:

1. Find an aquarium or bird sanctuary near you.
2. Research cost and transportation.
3. Choose a date.
4. Enjoy up-close encounters with wildlife!
5. Do a post field-trip review.

Tennessee: Tennessee Aquarium (Chattanooga)

SOUTHWEST

Texas: Downtown Aquarium (Houston), Dallas World Aquarium (Dallas), Texas State Aquarium (Corpus Christi), Moody Gardens (Galveston)

WEST

Alaska: Alaska Sealife Center (Seward)

California: Aquarium of the Pacific (Long Beach), Steinhart Aquarium (San Francisco), Monterey Bay Aquarium (Monterey)

Colorado: Downtown Aquarium (Denver)

Hawaii: Waikiki Aquarium (Honolulu)

Oregon: Oregon Coast Aquarium (Newport)

Suggestions for birding field trips: Visit the National Audubon Society's website for bird-watching tips, bird guides, and state-by-state birding suggestions. Or check out some of the popular birding sites below.

NORTHEAST

Maine: Mount Desert Island

Massachusetts: Quabbin Reservoir, Cape Cod National Sea Shore

New Jersey: Cape May Point

New York: Central Park

Pennsylvania: Hawk Mountain Sanctuary (Kempton)

MIDWEST

Kansas: Cheyenne Bottoms Wildlife Management Area (Great Bend)

Minnesota: Tamarac National Wildlife Refuge (Rochert)

Missouri: Greer Spring National Natural Landmark (Woodside Township)

Ohio: Magee Marsh (Oregon)

MOUNTAIN STATES

Colorado: Barr Lake State Park, Pawnee National Grassland

Utah: Bear River Migratory Bird Refuge

SOUTHEAST

Alabama: Dauphin Island

Florida: Everglades National Park (Homestead), Biscayne National Park

Louisiana: Grand Isle

Maryland: Blackwater National Wildlife Refuge (Cambridge)

SOUTHWEST

Arizona: Cave Creek Canyon (Portal), Paton Center for Hummingbirds (Patagonia)

New Mexico: Bosque del Apache National Wildlife Refuge

Texas: Aransas National Wildlife Refuge (Port Lavaca), Balcones Canyonlands National Wildlife Refuge (Marble Falls), Bolivar Flats Shorebird Sanctuary (Port Bolivar), Estero Llano Grande State Park (Weslaco)

WEST

Alaska: Denali National Park

California: Tule Lake, Yosemite National Park (Merced), Monterey Peninsula

Wyoming: Grand Teton National Park (Jackson)

27

Blueberry Hill

Family relationships have led to unexpected field trips—some requiring talent I didn't think I had! When my daughter Michaela was around ten years old, she had an audition for a production of *A Charles Dickens Christmas*. While I waited for her in the lobby, a grand dame of the theater approached me. "What part are you auditioning for?"

"This is a musical, isn't it?"

"Yes."

"My idea of singing in public is me singing alone in my car during rush hour."

Undeterred by my joke, the woman poked her head into the theater and yelled, "Dave, do we have any non-singing roles?"

Someone inside shouted, "Yes!"

She waved me toward the door. "We have non-singing roles! Get out there and read for a part!"

I knew I could read lines—my radio experience taught me how to enunciate properly—and I didn't fear public speaking. Plus, the older woman's hopeful encouragement tugged at me. How could I say no to such a passionate theater professional?

"Ooookay," I said, and headed into the auditorium.

Can you believe the director cast both Michaela and me?! Michaela won a great part and I picked up several bit roles. The director also coerced me into singing with the chorus.

During the rehearsals and performances, I had a blast belting out songs like a chorus champ. Did I sound good? I doubt it! But singing in that show was a groundbreaking field trip.

Though a competitor in sports and business, I'd only dabbled in music by banging on my dad's old drum set. While I loved to whale on those drums and did develop enough stick skills to play in the school band, I never took music seriously. But my choral performance reminded me how much I enjoyed singing and gave me confidence to do it at other venues.

Before the play, I only ever sang with my Uncle Roger. A fantastic guy who never had kids of his own, he always played a big part in his sisters' families. He brought me to my first two Red Sox games at Fenway Park, took me to University of Connecticut basketball games, and gave me my first job. At some point, Uncle Rog and I started singing Fat's Domino's famous "Blueberry Hill" at family gatherings.

No one would have picked either of us in a sing-off, but we didn't care. We sang so loudly, no one could escape our duet. They just laughed.

When my uncle passed away, I spoke at his service. After I said a few words about how important he was to me and his family, I started singing "Blueberry Hill" in front of the crowded church. Our family joined in and the decibels rose. Together, we raised our voices, reliving the joy Uncle Rog had given us.

A few months later, I was in Ireland to deliver a training program. The night before, I dined at a local pub with corporate staff members. While we enjoyed a great meal, I heard others singing "Molly Malone" in the next room:

In Dublin's fair city
Where the girls are so pretty
I first set my eyes on sweet Molly Malone
As she wheeled her wheelbarrow
Through the streets broad and narrow
Crying "cockles and mussels, alive, alive, oh"
Alive, alive, oh
Alive, alive, oh
Crying "cockles and mussels, alive, alive, oh"
She was a fishmonger
And sure, 'twas no wonder
For so were her mother and father before
And they wheeled their barrow
Through the streets broad and narrow
Crying "cockles and mussels, alive, alive, oh"
Alive, alive, oh
Alive, alive, oh
Crying "cockles and mussels, alive, alive, oh"
She died of a fever
And sure, so one could save her
And that was the end of sweet Molly...

I wrote down the lyrics and had copies printed at the hotel front desk. The next day, at my direction, all fifty training-program participants stood up and sang "Molly Malone." It put zip in everyone's step and kicked off the morning on a high note!

You don't have to have superstar talent to do something you enjoy. For your next field trip, tune out your inner critic and warm up those vocal cords. Go solo, grab a partner, or join the chorus and sing!

FIELD TRIP:

Get out there and sing!

Field Trip Challenge: Lift your voice and other people's spirits—find a music group that performs at nursing homes in your area.

SUGGESTIONS FOR SINGING FIELD TRIPS:

Go to karaoke nights weekly.

Take voice lessons online or in person.

Join a choir or an acapella group.

Start a band.

Sing out loud every day without apology.

Audition at a community theater.

Call-To-Action Plan:

1. Find music you love.
2. Practice in the shower or your car!
3. Choose a singing activity.
4. Go, do it, and have fun!
5. Do a post field-trip review.

28

Determined to Play

Field-trip obstacles abound—but there's always a way around them if you ask yourself, "How can I create some fun?"

My daughter Caitlin kept up a regular workout schedule in college, but she knew Thanksgiving break meant frantic holiday shopping, continuous eating, and little time for exercise field trips. Determined to enjoy the holiday, she asked herself: How can I have fun, spend quality time with my family, and still stay physically active?

The Kennedy family gave her an idea.

"Hey, I think it'd be fun to play a family football game tomorrow—just like the Kennedys," she announced the night before turkey day. "The weather will be cold but nice, and everyone could use a workout before gorging themselves. Whadduya think?"

"Sounds fun!" I said.

"I'll be the quarterback," Kevin volunteered.

"Good! Then I'll get to sack you," Michaela scoffed.

"Seems like your idea is already a hit," Helen quipped.

"Okay good!" Caitlin laughed. "I'll call everyone tonight and tell them the plan. Maybe I'll even suggest they dress the part—you know, wear their favorite team's colors. Do we have blue and gold face paint? I'm goin' all out."

Everyone came ready to play the next day. The college girls wore their school colors and painted their faces to match. The boys dressed in National Football League jerseys with the names and numbers of their favorite players.

"Let's get this started!" Uncle Steve exclaimed, leading us outside. "I'm gonna pick the teams so we can have a competitive game."

"I wanna be quarterback!" Kevin announced.

"I'm gonna quarterback for both sides," Uncle Steve declared. "I'm the only one here who's ever played football!"

Once the game started, the girls kept it light and fun, but the high-school boys acted like they were competing for a big-time college scholarship. After one play got out of hand, Uncle Steve called "time."

"Hey Coach Jay, I think we need a ref to keep this competition friendly. You mind?"

"Not at all," I said.

A few penalties later, the boys settled down and even let younger family members carry the ball.

By all measures, the game was a huge success. Everyone had a blast, burned off some calories, and felt like hungry warriors when they finally sat down to eat.

An hour-and-a-half after the meal, Caitlin rallied the troops off the couch. "I'm heading out for a walk around the neighborhood. Who's with me?"

Everyone immediately went looking for their jackets. Even the uncles who had nodded off after watching the Lions take another one on the chin grudgingly got up.

Outside, I felt glad to shake off the turkey coma in the cold, fresh air. And walking the neighborhood with so many family members felt like another wonderful field trip.

Later that night after everyone left, I put my arm around Caitlin. "Today was awesome. Thanks for organizing the game and the walk."

"You're welcome, Dad. It was fun. Think we should do it again next year?"

"Absolutely—a new holiday tradition!"

Caitlin's efforts reminded me of another person who seemed equally determined to enjoy field trips despite obstacles.

On another cold day, I struck up a conversation with John, a fellow skier, as we shared a chairlift to the top of Wachusett Mountain.

"Great day," I said.

"I wouldn't mind a few degrees warmer," the elderly gentleman replied.

"You chose to live in New England!"

"Sure, but it's only eight degrees. Where's the global warming?"

"I'm not sure how to dress for skiing when it's warm," I chuckled.

"I ski eighty times a year, so I'm on the slopes through March. It's easy to know how to dress—just wear fewer layers."

"Eighty times a year! You retired?"

"Kind of. I have the best of both worlds. I ski all winter and work as a golf ranger and play golf the rest of the year."

"Good living indeed! Not tempted to move to the Sun Belt?"

"Nah. I'd miss the snow. Besides, that's what old people do. I don't feel seventy-one, and I wanna keep it that way."

Wow! John was seventy-one years young in my book and, from the sound of things, a kindred spirit. Even in eight-degree weather, he headed outside for a multi-dimensional field trip that included fresh air, nature, exercise, and social interaction. He didn't let cold—or age—prevent him from having fun.

Weekday mornings at Wachusett Mountain, I see a lot of elderly skiers struggling to walk through the lodge in their stiff, heavy ski boots. But when they get out on the slopes—look out! They can really bring it!

These folks always remind me of the 1985 movie Cocoon, a charming sci-fi story about rest home residents who discovered a neighboring pool had turned into a fountain of youth. After swimming in its restorative waters, the residents felt young again and resumed the activities age had forced them to give up.

The seniors I see at Wachusett Mountain might love a dip in the fountain of youth, but lacking one, they layer up, snap on their skis, and schuss their way down the mountain. Wahoo! Those "Cocooners" (as I call them) can really fly!

Don't let weather—or anything else—turn you into a couch potato. Obstacles are field-trip opportunities if you believe—like I do—there's always a way to play.

FIELD TRIP:

Try a cold (or hot)—climate activity!

Field Trip Challenge (Cold Climate):

Go all in and buy a season pass to a nearby ski area! Like John, you'll get big value and lots of field-trip dates. The Epic and Ikon passes have optional plans for many resorts across the country. The Mountain Collective Pass includes eighteen mountains in the western U.S. and Canada.

Call-To-Action Plan:

1. Choose an activity.
2. Research where to go and what you'll need for gear.
3. Rent or purchase gear.
4. Make sure conditions are suitable.
5. Do a post field-trip review.

Field Trip Challenge (Hot Climate): Live in a warm

climate? Get a season pass to an amusement park! The big parks (Disney, Universal, and Six Flags) all offer great deals for pass holders as do the smaller parks around the U.S.

SUGGESTIONS FOR COLD-CLIMATE FIELD TRIPS:

Cross-Country Skiing: Experience nature's winter wonderland and get a great cardio workout. You'll be amazed at the number of trails available.

Downhill Skiing: This activity is such an adrenaline rush, you'll be singing "Let It Snow!" all winter. If Mother Nature doesn't provide, no worries—resorts make snow to keep their mountains operational.

Ice Skating: See if there's a local rink with open skating time. If you live near a pond or lake, clear off the snow and give it a go! But be careful—only skate outside when the temperatures have been consistently below freezing and you're sure the ice can safely support your weight.

Sledding: This childhood activity just never gets old—and it's basically free! Dig out your old sled, borrow one from a neighbor, or use a cafeteria tray like the college kids do. Then find a great hill and—whoosh—enjoy the ride!

Snowboarding: Developed in the 1960s, this relative newcomer to the winter sports scene drew its inspiration from skateboarding, sledding, downhill skiing, and surfing. Skiers and snowboarders share the slopes at almost all ski resorts.

Snowmobiling: With these motorized sleds, you can speed along established trails. In Maine alone, you can ride from region to region on 4,000 miles of primary trails known as the Interconnected Trail System (ITS).

Snowshoeing: Deep snow can be an obstacle, but snowshoes prevent you from sinking down. Strap them on and be the first to carve a path through the snowy woods.

Snow Tubing: If your local sledding hill doesn't provide enough thrills, find a resort where you can ride inflatable tubes down long, snowy inclines.

Winter Hiking: People like me who love the mountains hike all-year round. In fact, author Tom Ryan wrote about his attempt to hike all of New Hampshire's 4,000-foot mountains twice during one winter in his book Following Atticus: Forty-eight Peaks, One Little Dog, and an Extraordinary Friendship.

SUGGESTIONS FOR HOT-CLIMATE FIELD TRIPS:

All-Terrain Vehicle (ATV) Riding: With ATV trails is all fifty states, you can plan off-road adventures all year round.

Rollerblading: Who needs ice when you can glide anywhere on wheels?

Sand Sledding or Boarding: Believe it or not, this activity dates back to ancient Egypt but started becoming popular in the U.S. around the 1960s. Try it anywhere there are significant dunes—Colorado, Oregon, Texas, California, New Mexico, and North Carolina. If sand isn't your thing, consider surfing or skateboarding.

Waterskiing: If taking your usual dip doesn't excite you, try skimming along the water's surface on skis.

Water Tubing: Enjoy this fun water activity two ways: free float down a river or tether an inner tube to a boat and let it whisk you along.

29

Catching the Sun

Traveling to far-away places isn't always possible, but field trips can still happen everywhere and every day.

There are no mountains between my home and the Atlantic Ocean, so we get to see the sun rise every cloudless morning. While it's always beautiful, I've noticed it's particularly stunning in winter and early spring because the crisp air makes the colors more vibrant. Waking up early on those mornings—and others in summer and fall—lets me experience a field trip right outside my door. That's a simple joy I don't take for granted.

But sunsets are a different story in more ways than one. They're not easily seen from my house, so we have to go elsewhere to catch one—and since the family is up and about, they aren't peaceful, solo experiences. We're always looking to liven things up, and sunsets are no different.

Years ago, when we positioned ourselves on a beautiful Nantucket Island beach just to watch the sun sink below the horizon, the kids and I engaged in a stone-skimming challenge. All was well until Michaela bent over to pick up a rock and Kevin sent his stone speeding over her. When she stood up, the rock sliced her ear.

Needless to say, that sunset experience ended in the emergency room.

But other evening outings had happier endings. Seeing pink and orange light bounce off a snowy Grand Canyon was a magical experience. In Death Valley National Park, we marveled at even more intense colors—deep red and gold clouds swirled over purplish dunes. Incredible!

Sunset field trips and easy hikes were part of every family vacation, so my children now share my enthusiasm for the outdoors. Even so, I was still surprised—and overwhelmingly proud—when they asked me to lead a sunset hike up New Hampshire's Mt. Monadnock.

Starting at about 6:30 p.m., we took the long route, enjoying each other's company and conversation as well as spectacular views along the way. On the summit, we chatted with other groups and nibbled on snacks as the sun's magical fire cascaded down the mountainside. We took many Instagram-worthy photos and stayed until the sun disappeared.

When we put on our headlamps to safely navigate our descent, I realized the kids were getting a field trip within a field trip.

"I'm hearing the woods," Michaela said, obviously noticing sounds she had missed during the daylight trek.

Her comment reminded me of something, and turning to Kevin, I said, "Let's use our headlamps to see into the woods, just like we did on our moosing trip."

"Great idea, Dad! That so was cool seeing moose eyes staring out from the trees."

Though we'd occasionally stop to swivel our heads to either side of the trail, none of us saw any nocturnal creatures. That's okay—we still had fun! More importantly, the kids realized that headlamps make mountain field trips accessible after dark.

About two weeks after that sunset hike, my daughters did one on their own. Now they have a lifetime of night treks ahead of them.

And so do you! Like I've said from the beginning, field trips are everywhere—make it a priority to take one every day and before long, you'll see that every day is a field trip.

Watch the sun rise or set!

Suggestions for Sunrise Field Trips: Go to one of the following locations if and when you can or watch the sun rise anywhere in your town.

NORTHEAST

Maine: Acadia National Park. Be the first in the country to see the sunrise from Cadillac Mountain.

Massachusetts: Lighthouse Beach, Chatham. When the sun rises, it feels as if you're standing on the edge of the earth.

New York: Central Park, New York City. Early morning joggers and walkers have a front-row view. Fire Island. See the really cool Fire Island Lighthouse Tower at the same time.

MIDWEST

Kansas: Flint Hills.

SOUTHEAST

Florida: Key West. Renowned for its sunsets, this island also hails supreme for sunrises. Canaveral National Seashore. Thank goodness for the space program! The government protected 58,000 acres of seashore to prevent development too close to rocket launches. A true Florida sunrise without buildings nearby.

Georgia: North Beach, Tybee Island, Chatham County.

Call-To-Action Plan:

1. Look up times for sunrise or sunset.

2. Set your alarm so you don't miss your appointment with the sun!

3. Invite family or friends to share the experience.

4. Do a post field-trip review.

Maryland: Druid Hill Park, Baltimore. Sunrise reflects off the lake.

North Carolina: Cape Hatteras National Seashore. North Carolina's easternmost point.

Virginia: Ravens Roost Overlook, Lyndhurst. On the Blue Ridge Parkway.

Washington D.C.: National Mall. I have my daughter Caitlin to thank for this one. We went early during cherry blossom season to see the sun rise over the Basin.

SOUTHWEST

Arizona: Grand Canyon. An array of color blasts throughout the canyon walls. I was lucky enough to have snow during my visit. Saguaro National Park. Bright orange blazes behind the silhouettes of its namesake cacti.

WEST

California: Yosemite National Park. Views over Half Dome. Death Valley National Park, from Zabriskie Point.

Colorado: Lookout Mountain. Drive up the 7,377-foot mountain overlooking Denver.

Hawaii: Mt. Haleakala, Maui. Simply Spectacular.

Oregon: Powell Butte Nature Park, Portland. Within Portland's city limits.

South Dakota: Badlands National Park, Solitude.

Utah: Bryce Canyon. I know, another national park. They have it all!

Washington: Mt. Rainier. View the sun rising over the Cascades.

Suggestions for Sunset Field Trips: Bring a drink to sip as you watch the sun slip below the horizon at one of these cool places or anywhere near you.

NORTHEAST

Massachusetts: Aquinnah, Martha's Vineyard. Fort Tabor, Fort Rodman, New Bedford.

New York: Pebble Beach, Brooklyn.

MIDWEST

Minnesota: Burntside Lake, Ely. Red Jacket Trail, Mankato.

SOUTHEAST

Florida: Mallory Square, Key West. Everglades National Park. Four Seasons Hotel, Miami.

North Carolina: Outer Banks.

SOUTHWEST

Arizona: Hopi Point, Grand Canyon.

New Mexico: Old Fort Marcy Park, Santa Fe. Ojito Wilderness.

WEST

Alaska: Denali National Park. Glacier Bay National Park.

California: Laguna Beach. Santa Monica Pier. Treasure Island (near the Bay Bridge in San Francisco). Santa Barbara.

Colorado: John Martin Reservoir State Park, Hasty.

Hawaii: Haleakala, Maui. Kailua-Kona, Big Island.

Utah: Ensign Peak. Delicate Arch hike, Moab.

Washington: Orcas Island. Carkeek Park, Seattle.

Wyoming: Grand Tetons National Park.

PART 4

Field Trips to Challenge Yourself

Ever since I was a kid, I looked for ways to maximize my field-trip opportunities.

The more I pushed myself to get out there, the more I saw, tasted, experienced, and loved!

Along the way, I encountered kindred spirits who inspired me to expand my play zone. I also witnessed other field-trip companions battle fear so they could experience something new and wonderful. Their willingness to challenge themselves amazed me, and I felt their discovery joy as if it were my own.

The world is full of fun if we let go of our limits, put ourselves out there, and make enjoying life a priority.

Don't just make your bucket list—get it done! And keep adding to it!

30

Yikes!

My competitive spirit kicks in whenever I set an inspiring field-trip goal. Once I decide on a challenge, I set in motion a personal drama that ends in one of two ways: either I'll toast a new victory or eat some humble pie. But no matter how the story ends, the field trip is always worth my while!

Biking is one of my favorite forms of exercise because it doesn't hurt and it's totally controllable. I can go fast or slow, climb hills, or glide along straightaways. I can take a short jaunt or push myself to do a 100-mile Century ride.

I once took a bike ride in the hills of central Massachusetts. I hadn't decided how to challenge myself because I was too busy enjoying the spectacular autumn scenery. Red, yellow, and orange leaves popped against dark-emerald evergreens as I rode along winding, country roads. But about mile twenty, I found my challenge when I saw another rider three-quarters of the way up a steep, mile-long hill ahead of me.

I'm gonna catch that rider before he reaches the top, I told myself. Putting my head down and pedaling furiously, I charged uphill. Just before the top, I caught up with him and silently celebrated my little victory.

"Nice day, isn't it?" I said.

"Sure is," he replied. "I love this time of year."

"Me, too. I cringe if I have to leave New England during the fall."

"Where you riding to?"

"Haven't decided yet. I've already done twenty, but it's so nice, I'm thinking I might ride for another twenty. Where are you headed?"

"I'm finishing up a sixty-mile ride. My house is just up the street about a mile or so."

Holy cow! I thought. I'd been congratulating myself for catching up to a guy who had already pedaled forty miles more than me. Then he dropped another question: "How old are you?"

"Fifty-four."

"I'm seventy-four."

Yay me—I caught up with a guy twenty years my senior at the end of his sixty-mile ride. Despite my deflated ego, I found my fellow rider's not-so-subtle point amusing. Then I watched as he went into his final-leg kick and pulled ahead. Whoa, this guy still has it!

I rose to the challenge, pedaled faster, and moved out in front. We kept pace with each other, each determined not to let the other guy get the satisfaction of winning.

What a field trip for us two geezers!

My fellow biker slowed down as he pulled off to his house, but I continued on totally pumped. Not only did he leave me with great motivation for biking another forty miles, he showed me I had at least another twenty good years of biking ahead of me.

My humble pie came heaped with vanilla ice cream!

That glorious day I thought about how bikes had evolved since they were invented in 1817. The first cruisers were designed for transportation, but later iterations—ten-speeds, BMX, mountain, and fat-tire bikes—became the rage when people figured out how much fun biking could be.

Biking enthusiasts eventually joined forces with walkers, railroad-history buffs, and conservationists to turn unused railroad corridors into public trails. Today more than 21,000 miles of rail-trails provide safe spaces for Americans to walk, run, hike, skate, and bike.

You know where I'm going with this, right? Dust off your two-wheeler, pump up the tires, and explore a rail trail! Reconnect with the exhilaration you felt as a kid when you took off on your first set of wheels. Then set yourself a fun challenge. Five miles? Ten? Twenty-five?

Where you start doesn't matter. The more biking field trips you take, the farther you'll go and the more fun you'll have.

Get out there—nature and adventure await!

FIELD TRIP:

Take a bike ride on a rail-trail!

Field Trip Challenge: Make it a goal to ride a rail-trail from end-to-end!

Suggestions for Rail Trails: There are so many trails across the country! My favorites are listed below along with some famous ones. For more detailed information about rail trails near you, visit railstotrails.org or trailing.com.

Call-To-Action Plan:

1. Find a rail-trail near you.
2. Invite friends or family.
3. Prep your bike for a long ride.
4. Pack water!
5. Do a post field-trip review.

NORTHEAST

Connecticut: Farmington Canal Heritage Trail (New Haven)

Delaware: Southern Delaware Heritage Bike Trail

Maine: Eastern Trail (Kittery)

Maryland: C & O Canal Trail (Cumberland)

Massachusetts: Cape Cod Rail Trail, Charles River Bike Path (Boston)

New Hampshire: Great Glen Trails (Gorham)

New Jersey: Delaware and Raritan Canal State Park (Stockton)

New York: Hudson River Greenway (New York City), High Line (No bikes, New York City), South County Trailway (Yonkers), The Erie Canalway Trail (Albany)

Pennsylvania: Three Rivers Heritage Trail (Pittsburgh), Great Allegheny Passage (Homestead)

Rhode Island: East Bay Bike Path (Bristol)

Vermont: Island Line Trail (Burlington)

MIDWEST

Indiana: Cardinal Greenways Trail (Muncie)

Illinois: Chicago Lakefront Trail, The 606 (Chicago), Des Plaines River Trail (Wadsworth)

Iowa: High Trestle Trail (Ankeny)

Kansas: Prairie Spirit Rail Trail (Ottawa)

Kentucky: Louisville Riverwalk (Louisville)

Michigan: North Central State Trail (Gaylord)

Minnesota: Mesabi Trail (Ely)

Missouri: Katy Trail (Machens)

Nebraska: The Cowboy and Recreation and Nature Trail (Valentine)

Ohio: Ohio to Erie Trail (Cincinnati to Cleveland), Alum Creek Greenway Trail (Columbus/ Westerville)

Oklahoma: The Oklahoma River Trail (Oklahoma City)

Wisconsin: CAMBA (Hayward)

SOUTHEAST

Alabama: Chief Ladiga Trail (Anniston)

Arkansas: Arkansas River Trail (Little Rock)

Florida: Shark Valley Trail (Everglades National Park)

Georgia: Atlanta Beltline, Silver Comet Trail (Smyrna)

Louisiana: Tammany Trace (Mandeville)

Mississippi: Longleaf Trace (Hattiesburg)

North Carolina: River To sea Bikeway (Wilmington)

South Carolina: Huntington Beach State Park Path (Murrells Inlet)

Virginia: The Virginia Creeper Trail (Abingdon)

Washington D.C.: Mount Vernon Trail

West Virginia: Greenbrier River Trail (Caldwell)

SOUTHWEST

Arizona: The Loop (Tucson), The Arizona Trail

New Mexico: Cloud Climbing Rail Trail (Cloudcroft)

Texas: Ann and Roy Butler Hike and Bike Trail (Austin), River Legacy Trail (Arlington), Buffalo Bayou Hike and Bike Trail (Houston), Fresno-Sauceda Loop (Big Bend Ranch State Park)

WEST

Alaska: SEAtrails (Yakutat)

California: Griffith Park (Los Angeles), Metro Orange Line Bike Path (Los Angeles), San Gabriel River Trail (Los Angeles), The Strand (Southern California), The Presidio (San Francisco), Mt. Tamalpais (Mill Valley), Tennessee Valley Trail and Muir Woods (San Francisco).

Colorado: The Colorado Trail (Denver)

Hawaii: Awa'awapuhi Trail (Waimea)

Idaho: Trail of the Coeur d'Alenes (Cataldo), Route of the Hiawatha (Wallace)

Nevada: The Flume Trail (Glenbrook)

North Dakota: Math Dash Hey Trail (Medora)

Oregon: Willamette River Loop (Portland), Row River Trail (Cottage Grove)

South Dakota: George S. Mickelson Trail (Edgemont)

Utah: Moab Canyon Pathway (Moab)

Washington: Burke-Gilman Trail (Seattle)

Wyoming: The Pathway (Jackson Hole and the Grand Tetons), Medicine Bow Rail-Trail (Lake Owen)

31

Fear of Heights

Not everyone takes a field trip to have fun. Some folks sign up for a challenging adventure to see what's on the other side of fear. Those who push through it are often rewarded with an amazing view, thrill-ride exhilaration, and maybe even boundary-smashing personal growth.

The company I worked for had a hot-air balloon logo with its name in large letters in the middle. We periodically organized events to give the logo "airtime" over the New England skies. We'd offer rides in a tethered balloon or ask Chris, our balloon pilot, to float the logo and a few guests around the region.

I'd seen Chris in action on more than one occasion. He asked potential riders to show up at dawn or dusk, when the wind is lighter. After testing the wind, he would tell us whether we could fly. If he declared a no-go, people were naturally disappointed. But he would tell them, "You're right where you need to be. Better to be on the ground wishing you were in the air, then in the air wishing you were on the ground."

On the day I invited my moosing friend Steve for a ride, the wind was calm, and Chris gave us the go sign. We stepped into the basket and started floating above the ground.

"Where should I stand?" Steve asked nervously. "It feels like I could fall out."

"Yeah, tall people sometimes feel that way because the basket only reaches their waist," Chris replied. "Try standing closer to the middle... or do you have an issue with heights?"

Steve nodded.

"Then the only place you'll feel comfortable is sitting on the floor. You can't see how high we are from there."

I was stunned by my friend's admission. "If you're afraid of heights, why are you in this balloon?"

"I wanted to face my fear and overcome it."

"Wow. Good for you. I'm impressed. Just do whatever you need to do to feel comfortable."

He knelt down and gripped the edge of the basket. "How does this thing fly?" he asked.

"The balloon floats because hot air rises," Chris explained. "The fire heats the air inside the balloon. When it becomes lighter than the outside air, the balloon floats up. If I wanna go higher, I add heat. When I wanna descend, I tone it down."

Chris continued talking. He seemed to know it had a calming effect on nervous passengers. "Did you know there's a ballooning tradition involving champagne?"

"Champagne! Don't tell me people actually drink when they're in these things!"

"No, no, they don't," Chris assured him. "The first balloon voyage took place back in 1783 in Paris, France. Just imagine how frightening it was for farmers to see a giant balloon descending out of the sky. And they probably weren't happy when it landed in the middle of their crops. So, ballooners used to bring champagne as a peace offering. We still honor that tradition by sharing a champagne toast after we land."

Either the storytelling or the promise of champagne eased Steve's nerves enough for him to stand up. "How high are we now?"

"About a thousand feet."

"Amazing. When you get used to it, it's actually kind of magical floating over the treetops like a giant bird... Hey, look—people!" Waving to those on the ground, Steve shouted, "We're off to see the Wizard of Oz! Have you seen the yellow brick road?"

I grinned at his excitement, glad that he hadn't let his fear of heights ruin a spectacular field trip.

The experience reminded me of when I took my family to Willis Tower in Chicago. The 103rd floor has clear observation boxes that extend out, so it feels like you're walking on air at 1,353 feet. My kids jumped right onto the glass floor, but an adult in another party had to crawl out on all fours. I couldn't help admiring her determination to fully experience that field trip despite her fear of heights.

I felt the same way when my colleague Jack pushed through his fear at a company rock-climbing event with Outward Bound. Though visibly shaking, he walked to the ledge and rappelled down a seventy-foot cliff. I could only imagine the exuberance he felt when he reached the bottom.

Field trips that challenge us offer more than a momentary thrill. They show us the depths of our courage and—like balloon rides, tall buildings, and rock climbing—a landscape of infinite possibility.

FIELD TRIP:

Get off the ground!

Field Trip Challenge: Go for the trifecta—do a field trip in each of the three categories below!

Suggestions for balloon field trips: Find a hot-air balloon festival near you. Go as a spectator or take part in flights or tethered rides. If you don't want to wait for a festival, Google balloon rides for sale.

NORTHEAST

Maine: Great Falls Balloon Festival

New Jersey: Quick Check Festival of Ballooning, Warren County Farmers Fair Balloon Festival

New York: Adirondack Hot Air Balloon Festival, Spiedie Fest & Balloon Rally, Hudson Valley Hot Air Balloon Festival, Great Wellsville Balloon Rally

Call-To-Action Plan:

1. **Choose an adventure that gets you off the ground.**

2. **If this is hard for you, invite supportive friends.**

3. **Set the date and get tickets.**

4. **Enjoy the view!**

5. **Do a post field-trip review.**

Pennsylvania: Chester County Balloon Festival, Thurston Classic

Vermont: Quechee Hot Air Balloon Craft & Music Festival

MIDWEST

Illinois: Centralia Balloon Festival, Lisle Eye to the Skies Festival

Iowa: National Balloon Classic, National Balloon Classic Field

Michigan: Field of Flight Air Show and Balloon Festival, Hot Air Jubilee

Missouri: Great Forest Park Balloon Race, Great Pershing Balloon Derby

Ohio: Ashland BalloonFest, Ravenna Balloon-A-Fair

SOUTHEAST

Alabama: Alabama Jubilee Hot Air Balloon Classic

Georgia: Helen to the Atlantic Balloon Race and Festival

Mississippi: Great Mississippi River Balloon Race

North Carolina: Carolina BalloonFest

South Carolina: Freedom Aloft Weekend

Tennessee: Lakeside of the Smokies Balloon Fest

West Virginia: University Toyota's Balloons over Morgantown

SOUTHWEST

Arizona: Havasu Balloon Festival and Fair, Colorado River Crossing Balloon Festival

New Mexico: Albuquerque International Balloon Fiesta

Texas: Great Texas Balloon Race

WEST

California: Sonoma County Hot Air Balloon Classic, Temecula Valley Balloon and Wine Festival, Temecula Valley Balloon & Wine Classic

Colorado: Colorado Springs Labor Day Lift Off

Idaho: Teton Valley Balloon Rally, Spirit of Boise Balloon Rally

Nevada: The Great Reno Balloon Race

Oregon: Northwest Art & Air Festival

Utah: Bluff Balloon Festival, Eyes to the Sky Balloon Festival

Washington: Great Prosser Balloon Rally

SUGGESTIONS FOR OBSERVATION-DECK FIELD TRIPS IN NORTH AMERICA:

NORTHEAST

Canada: CN Tower (Toronto)

New York: Empire State Building (New York City), Top of the Rock (New York City)

Washington, D.C.: Washington Monument

MIDWEST

Canada: Calgary Tower (Calgary, Alberta), Glacier Skywalk (Banff, Alberta)

Kentucky: Jefferson Davis Monument (Fairview)

Minnesota: Enger Tower (Duluth)

Missouri: Gateway Arch (St. Louis)

Wisconsin: The Infinity Room at the House on the Rock (Spring Green)

SOUTHEAST

Tennessee: Clingmans Dome Observation Tower (Great Smoky Mountain National Park), Gatlinburg Space Needle (Gatlinburg)

SOUTHWEST

Arizona: Grand Canyon Skywalk (Peach Springs)

Texas: San Jacinto Monument (La Porte), Tower of the Americas (San Antonio), Reunion Tower (Dallas)

WEST

California: Theme Building Observation Deck (Los Angeles International Airport)

Nevada: Eiffel Tower (Las Vegas), Stratosphere Tower (Las Vegas)

Washington: Space Needle (Seattle)

Suggestions for rock-climbing field trips: Most REI stores have rock-climbing walls. You can sign up for a number of programs to learn before you commit to the sport as a regular activity. Or find a rock-climbing gym near you.

According to themanual.com, some of the best rock climbing in the world can be found at the following locales:

UNITED STATES

California: Yosemite National Park, Joshua Tree National Park

Kentucky: Red River Gorge

Maine: Acadia National Park

OUTSIDE THE U.S.

Greece: Kalymnos

Morocco: Todra Gorge

Thailand: Railay Beach

32

Split

Challenging field trips come in all forms. Some people who easily manage rappelling down a cliff can shrink back in terror when asked to dance. They fear looking bad in social situations. I got over that in high school when disco fever was really a thing.

Back then, a dance was already a not-to-be-missed field trip, but when the movie Saturday Night Fever became a monster hit, it turned disco into a movement. Even those like me who didn't love the music relished imitating Tony Manero, the film's smooth-moving disco star. We rocked our hips on the dance floor, jabbed our pointed fingers into the air, and had an absolute blast!

If we looked silly, the girls didn't care. They'd see us kicking it up and jump right in. Pretty soon, girls from other schools got in the groove. But the "cooler" guys never did. They watched from the sidelines.

In my senior year, I was invited to one of high school's biggest field trips—the junior prom. So much more than a high-school dance, the prom involved a complex series of interconnected field trips:

You had to take your date to dinner at a restaurant that required reservations.

You had to secure the one family car.

You had to dress up.

I didn't have money to buy a suit, so my Mom made me a cream-colored one that made me feel like a million bucks. Like a male version of Cinderella, I couldn't wait to make my entrance at the ball!

I picked up my date in our old Chrysler Newport, a boat on wheels. We double-dated with my sister and one of my best friends. Dining out was already a field trip since my family never ate in restaurants, but with close friends in killer outfits, it felt exponentially more fun.

By the time we entered University of Connecticut's student union ballroom, we were on an emotional high and ready to dance! My buddy and I twirled our dates into disco dips, and even did the Saturday Night Fever line dance known as the Brooklyn Shuffle. Then the DJ played "You Should Be Dancing"—the song where people in the movie clear the floor to watch Tony's moves and splits. Casting off any lingering limitations, I slid down into my own split. Rrrrrip! My pants burst at the seams and totally exposed my back side!

Cinderella didn't lose her gown until midnight, but there I was in tattered duds before the clock hit nine. Laughing hysterically, my friends hustled me off the dance floor.

"Should I just go home?" I asked.

"No, no, we'll figure this out," my buddy insisted. "Either of you girls sew?"

"I don't, but my sister does," my date volunteered. "Anyone have a dime for the pay phone?"

Lucky for me, the sister was home, so we hightailed it over to her house and she worked her magic. Thanks to my new fairy godmother, I was back at the ball in no time.

When the DJ played "Shout" by Otis Day and the Knights, we sprawled on the floor in our best version of The Worm. We twisted to Chubby Checker's "The Twist," rocked out to Bruce Springsteen's "Born to Run," then capped off the evening with a long slow dance to "Stairway to Heaven."

What a night!

Dancing is one of life's great pleasures, yet some of us don't do it because we can't shed our inhibitions. Even those of us who used to dance can feel self-conscious after a certain age. "I'll look ridiculous," we tell ourselves.

Having fun isn't ridiculous—it's infectious!

It's why professional sports venues encourage jumbotron dance-offs during timeouts. My son Kevin once earned major jumbotron time dance-battling another kid. As they took turns shaking everything they had in front of 18,000 fans, the crowds applauded and laughed. Everybody's joy-meter needle moved a little higher.

If it's been a while since you lit up the dance floor, then do I have a field trip for you! Shake off your insecurities, find a beat, and bust out those old moves—or learn some new ones. Just feel the music and dance!

FIELD TRIP:

Go dancing!

Field Trip Challenge:
Learn a new dance! Start with YouTube videos, connect with national dance studios like Fred Astaire or Arthur Murray, or find a local teacher. Not sure what dance to try? Consider these: bolero, cha cha, contra, country western, foxtrot, hustle, jive, mambo, merengue, paso doble, quickstep, rumba, salsa, samba, swing (east or west coast), tango, and waltz.

Call-To-Action Plan:
1. Find a dance partner.
2. Research dancing opportunities.
3. Put on your dancing shoes and go!
4. Do a post field-trip review.

SUGGESTIONS FOR DANCE FIELD TRIPS:

Boogie in your living room: If dancing seems like a difficult challenge, start small and build. Wait for everyone to leave the house, put on your favorite music, and let your wild self go free.

Dance at a club: When you're ready to practice your moves in public, find a nightlife venue that has music and a spacious dance floor.

Use MeetUp or other platforms to find your dance tribe: People organize dance events in local halls. Grab a partner and go!

Watch dancing movies to get inspired: Invite friends over, put on a great dance flick, and learn some hot moves from the greats. Movie suggestions: Saturday Night Fever, Flashdance, Strictly Ballroom, Footloose, Fame, Dirty Dancing, Billy Elliot, Step Up.

33

Brooklyn Bridge

Some field trips involve stepping out of your comfort zone, but others give you a reason to see more of what's out there.

I never really appreciated bridges until July 3, 1986, when three monumental occasions converged—the nation's 210th birthday, the Statue of Liberty's centennial anniversary, and the completion of her four-year renovation. President Ronald Reagan had invited French President Francois Mitterand to the unveiling ceremonies on July third, setting up a fantastic two-day party for the nation. A million-and-a-half people crowded into New York City for the celebration.

Since our office at One World Trade Center looked out at Lady Liberty, our company president decided to throw a party so the staff and their families could watch the big event.

I invited my mom. Not just because I thought she'd enjoy the party and pageantry, but I also wanted to introduce her to Helen. We'd only been dating a few months, but I was eager for them to meet. That big event went off without a hitch, and everyone enjoyed the party and unveiling ceremony.

"Hey, why don't we head down to the Brooklyn Bridge," I suggested. "We could get a closer look at the tall ships in the harbor."

"Sounds fun!" Helen agreed. "I've read it's supposed to be the largest flotilla of tall ships in modern history."

"Well, then, let's go!" Mom said.

The tall ships were as incredible as Lady Liberty's newly restored glory, but the view from the Brooklyn Bridge—which I'd driven over but never walked across—was just as memorable.

Looking back toward the city from the bridge, I spied the twin towers among lower Manhattan's skyscrapers. Wow, I thought, I work in a building that's part of that amazing, world-famous skyline! Then I looked uptown at the distinctive spires of the Empire State and Chrysler Buildings, the Manhattan Bridge, and all the way to Brooklyn, the Brooklyn Heights Promenade, and over to New York Harbor, the Statue of Liberty, and the Fulton St. dock.

On a day that already felt monumental, that stunning panorama made a powerful impression. From then on, I went out of my way to bring friends, family, colleagues, and customers to stand on that bridge and feel its magic.

When the travel baseball team I coached played a tournament in Queens, we stayed a few blocks from the bridge on the Brooklyn side, just so I could take the team on a bridge field trip. After we walked to Manhattan and back, we all enjoyed pizza at Grimaldi's, one of my favorite New York pizza joints near the bridge.

Over 10,000 pedestrians cross the Brooklyn Bridge every day. Who can blame them? How often do you get to combine exercise with breath-taking views of one of the world's greatest cities?

The Brooklyn Bridge inspired me to take on a new challenge—walk other cool bridges around the country. I created a bucket list of bridges and plan to work my way through it.

Care to join me? Just put on your walking shoes and set a fun goal! How many bridges can you explore in a month? A year?

Field-trip challenges don't always have to take place outside your comfort zone. Some only require a list, a plan, and a determination to see as many places as you can!

FIELD TRIP:
Walk bridges across the country!

Field Trip Challenge:
It's not possible to list all bridges here. With a little research, you can create your own list. Don't stop until you collect them all!

Suggestions for bridge field trips:

Call-To-Action Plan:
1. Create a plan to walk all the cool bridges in your region.
2. Take a selfie whenever you "collect" a bridge.
3. Keep going until you finish your list!
4. Do a post field-trip review.

NORTHEAST

Connecticut (Middletown and Portland): Arrigoni Bridge. This bridge not only has two distinctive steel arches reaching 600 feet, it carries the famous Route 66 over the Connecticut River.

Maine (Stockton Springs): Penobscot Narrows Bridge and Observatory. One of only two bridge observation towers in the world, this destination bridge allows visitors views of the Penobscot River, surrounding countryside, and distant mountains. It's location next to Fort Knox State Park lets you combine two cool field trips into one.

Massachusetts (Cambridge and Charlestown): North Bank Bridge. This pedestrian bridge connects Paul Revere Park in Charlestown to North Point Park in Cambridge. Two-hundred-ninety feet high and 690 feet long, it curves under the beautiful Zakim Bridge and gives you a great view as you ascend to the highest point.

Massachusetts (Shelburne Falls): The Bridge of Flowers. In 1928, when an old trolley bridge became useless, local resident Clara Barnard championed building gardens on the bridge. Today, visitors can walk among 500 varieties of flowers, vines, and shrubs planted to bloom continuously from April to October.

176

New York (New York City): Manhattan Bridge. Completed in 1909, this massive suspension bridge has seven lanes for cars, four for trains, one for bikes (on the bridge's north side), and a pedestrian walkway. The walkway is on the south side, so views include the Brooklyn Bridge, Statue of Liberty, lower Manhattan skyline, and New York Harbor.

New York (New York City): Williamsburg Bridge. This bridge was originally constructed for horse and carriage transportation in 1903. Enter at the lower east side of Manhattan and walk across to a great meal at Peter Lugers Steakhouse in Brooklyn.

New York (Poughkeepsie): Walkway over the Hudson. A railroad bridge converted into a rail trail, this 1.28-mile footpath extends over the Hudson River and connects Poughkeepsie to the town of Lloyd. Beautiful views of the Catskills and the Hudson Highlands abound. Keep the field trip going on the eighteen miles of rail trails that connect with the bridge.

Pennsylvania (Philadelphia) and New Jersey (Camden): Ben Franklin Bridge. Opened to traffic in 1926, this bridge's seven traffic lanes and pedestrian walkway cross over the Delaware River. Access to the bridge on the Philadelphia side is across the street from the U.S. Mint—another cool field trip!

Vermont and New Hampshire: Cornish-Windsor Bridge. This covered wooden bridge is not only the longest one in the U.S., it's the most prominent of all Vermont and New Hampshire's many covered bridges. If you're a big fan, stay in Vermont, which has the highest density of these quaint 19th-century structures or head to Pennsylvania, which has the most.

MIDWEST

Illinois (Chicago): BP Pedestrian Bridge. Is it a sculpture or a bridge? Both, I guess. Only two-tenths of a mile long, it connects Millennium Park and Maggie Daley Park over Columbus Drive. Enjoy views of the parks and Chicago's skyline.

Illinois (Chicago): DuSable Bridge. Opened to traffic in 1920, this trunnion bascule bridge can be raised so tall ships and boats traveling on the Chicago River can pass underneath. With its stunning views of the Chicago skyline, you may want to take your time crossing.

Indiana (Louisville and Jeffersonville): Big 4 Pedestrian Bridge. Spans the Ohio River one mile each way and delivers breathtaking views of the river, city, and waterfront park.

Kansas (Wichita): Keeper of the Plains Bridge. This cool bridge opened in January 2007. The South Bridge structure crosses the Arkansas River, while the North Bridge structure crosses the Little Arkansas River. The forty-four-foot-tall Keeper of the Plains sculpture created by artist Blackbear Bosin faces east at the confluence of the rivers.

Michigan (Mackinaw City and St. Ignace): Mackinac Bridge. The fifth-longest suspension bridge in the world, this bridge crosses over the straits of Mackinac and connects Michigan's upper and lower peninsulas. Between 25,000-57,000 people walk across during the annual Labor Day Bridge Walk every year.

Minnesota (Minneapolis): Lowry Avenue Bridge. One of the Twin Cities' twenty-three bridges that allows you to walk across the Mississippi River, its beautiful arches light up and reflect off the water at night.

Missouri (St. Louis) and Illinois (Madison): Chain of Rocks Bridge. A cool cantilever and truss bridge known for its sharp bend as it approaches land.

Ohio (Cincinnati) and Kentucky (Covington): John A. Roebling Suspension Bridge. Named after its architect, this was the longest suspension bridge in the world until Roebling's other masterwork—the Brooklyn Bridge—opened. Equally beautiful as its younger sibling, the Roebling Bridge entices pedestrians to cross the Ohio River on foot for their commute and cultural activities.

Ohio (Cincinnati) and Kentucky (Newport): Purple People Bridge. After enjoying a walk over the Ohio River on the Cincinnati side, you can pick up the 245-mile Ohio-to-Erie Trail all the way to Cleveland!

Nebraska (Omaha) and Iowa (Council Bluffs): Bob Kerrey Pedestrian Bridge. This 3,000-foot footbridge crosses the Missouri River and connects two states. Nature trails and parks on each side offer additional field trips.

Oklahoma (Oklahoma City): Skydance Bridge. This pedestrian-only bridge has a unique "V" shape that mimics the dance done by the Scissor-tailed Flycatcher (the state bird) while in flight. Soar over Interstate 40 on this public work of art!

SOUTHEAST

Alabama (Selma): Edmund Pettus Bridge. Part of the Selma-to-Montgomery National Historic trail, this bridge lets you relive history. Walk across to honor those Civil Rights demonstrators who died on Bloody Sunday (March 7, 1965).

Arkansas (Little Rock): Two Rivers Park Bridge. This 1,368-foot-long pedestrian and bike bridge leads to Two Rivers Park.

Georgia (Tallulah Falls): Tallulah Gorge Bridge. This pedestrian suspension bridge sways eighty feet above the Tallulah Gorge. The gorge is nearly one thousand feet deep and covers about two miles—a sight in itself and another great field trip.

North Carolina (Grandfather Mountain State Park): Mile High Swinging Bridge. The highest suspension footbridge in the country offers sweeping views of the park's mountain.

South Carolina (Charleston): Arthur Ravenel Jr. Bridge. A 2.7-mile bridge that spans from downtown Charleston to Mount Pleasant. Enjoy fantastic views of Charleston Harbor, the USS Yorktown, and downtown.

Tennessee (Gatlinburg): Skylift Bridge. This bridge rests on top of Crockett Mountain and on the edge of the Great Smoky Mountains National Park. A tourist attraction with ticket prices to match, this cool pedestrian-only bridge has glass panels so you can see the ground 140 feet below.

Tennessee (Nashville): John Seigenthaler Pedestrian Bridge. Great view of the Nashville skyline!

Washington, D.C.: Met Branch Trail Pedestrian Walkway. This bridge is part of the eight-mile Metropolitan Branch Trail that connects Silver Spring, Maryland, to Union Station in D.C. The bridge crosses over the rail tracks.

West Virginia (Fayetteville): New River Gorge Bridge. This twenty-four-inch-wide, 3,030-foot-long catwalk more than 850 feet above the river doesn't have room for two-way traffic, so visitors are shuttled back to the start.

SOUTHWEST

Arizona and Utah (Glen Canyon): Navajo Bridge. When a new bridge was constructed in 1995, they converted the old bridge to a pedestrian bridge. Now you can enjoy a walk at 467 feet over the Colorado River.

New Mexico (El Prado): Rio Grande Gorge Bridge (known locally as the Gorge Bridge or the High Bridge). Roughly six hundred feet above the Rio Grande, this steel deck arch bridge is the tenth-highest bridge in the United States.

Texas (Dallas): Ronald Kirk Bridge (formerly known as the Continental Avenue Bridge). The city turned this old bridge into a new footbridge/park where people can enjoy bocce courts, sit-down chess boards, human-sized chess boards, a playground, lounge chairs, and more. If that isn't enough, you can cross over to West Dallas and eat at Trinity Groves, a restaurant incubator with diverse restaurants and food choices that frequently change.

Texas (Dallas): Margaret Hunt Hill Bridge. Parallel to the Ronald Kirk Bridge, this vehicle bridge also has a pedestrian walkway leading to Trinity Groves. Its 40-foot arch with the Dallas skyline as a backdrop has become an Instagram-worthy photo shoot.

WEST

California (San Francisco): Golden Gate Bridge. A no brainer! When you visit San Francisco or Marin County, walk across the Golden Gate Bridge to see the Pacific Ocean on one side and San Francisco Bay on the other. On a clear day, take in views of the city skyline as well as Sausalito, Angel Island, and Alcatraz.

Colorado (Carson City): Royal Gorge Bridge & Park. A tourist attraction and part of a 360-acre amusement park, this bridge rises more than 900 feet above the Arkansas River and is currently the highest bridge in the United States. It extends 1,260 feet across the Royal Gorge.

Hawaii (Haleiwa and Oahu): Anahulu Stream Bridge. This narrow rainbow-arch bridge gets very busy. Walk across early in the morning or kayak in the Anahulu River and see it from the river below.

Idaho (Twin Falls): Perrine Bridge. This 1,500-foot-long bridge spans the Snake River Canyon. Thrill-seekers can indulge in a big, crazy field trip since it's legal to BASE jump from the bridge to the canyon floor. (BASE jumping is a recreational activity in which people parachute from high objects.)

Montana (Kootenai National Forest): Lake Koocanusa Bridge. This half-mile span rises more than 270 feet above Lake Koocanusa and offers excellent views of the lake.

Nevada-Arizona (Hoover Dam): Mike O'Callaghan-Pat Tillman Memorial Bridge. Soaring 900 feet over the Colorado River, this bridge connects Arizona and Nevada and is the second-highest bridge in the United States.

Oregon (Portland): Tilikum Crossing. Cross the Willamette River over this 1,700-foot long, cable-stayed bridge. The top cable's sloping angle mimics the slope of Mount Hood in the distance. Its LED lights change color based on the river's flow.

Washington (Seattle): West Thomas Street Pedestrian and Bicycle Overpass. A great elevated bike and pedestrian path built to connect the waterfront to city streets.

34

Rapids of Mayhem

S ome people sign up for challenging field trips without knowing what they're getting into. That happened to my buddy Mike when I asked if he wanted to join me and five other guys on my annual white-water rafting trip.

"Sure, I'll go," he said.

"You ever been rafting?"

"No, but I'll give it a try."

On a beautiful June day, we all arrived at the meeting spot for New England Outdoor Center, a white-water rafting company that offers guided trips down Maine's Penobscot River.

We had already donned our wetsuits and signed forms releasing the company from legal responsibility. Then the guide launched into the pre-trip safety talk.

"For those of you who've never done it before, white-water rafting is kinda like riding a roller coaster on water without a seatbelt or a safety bar. You can't be strapped in, because if the raft flips over, you'd drown."

"So, a rafter could fall out in the middle of the rapids?" Mike asked anxiously.

"Yes, and if that happens, you want to keep your feet up. You don't want them to get stuck in the rocks underneath. That's another way to drown."

"Has anyone ever died on one of these trips?"

"Not with our company, but yes, it has happened."

The color drained out of Mike's already-pale complexion.

"Now, if you do fall out, don't panic. Get your head above water as quickly as possible and face downstream. Just ride out the rapids until we can pull you out. Okay? Those of you who have more questions can hang back. The rest of you can grab a seat on the bus."

As our group waited to board, my buddy John razzed Mike. "Didn't Jay tell you to update your life insurance policy? Havin' second thoughts?"

Mike shook his head.

Did he regret coming along? I wondered. I thought about all the decisions he had to make just to get to this point:

He had to say yes to something he'd never even thought about doing.

He had to stay committed every time a naysayer said something like, "Are you crazy? I know someone who had a heart attack rafting and died."

He had to resist his own fear when he heard the guys telling rafting horror stories on the drive over and when he saw the risks detailed on the release form.

His bulging eyes told me he was fighting the urge to bail right now.

"Last one out of the river buys the beer!" one of the guys joked.

"Yeah, but what if Mike doesn't make it out?" another jibed.

"He'll make it just fine," I said. "I wouldn't risk one of the few decent hitters on our over-thirty baseball team if I thought otherwise."

Mike didn't react to any of the banter as we rode along the rough, dusty logging road through the Northwoods of Maine. We were so far from civilization the place didn't even have a town name—only a territory number. There was nothing but pure, breath-taking wilderness.

Inside the bus, the unpleasant smell of wetsuits mingled with a faint odor of sweat from forty or fifty people. I wondered what these adventurers— ranging from twenty- to seventy-years-old—were feeling as they headed toward their white-water field trip.

Some, like me, couldn't wait to zip through the heart-pounding Class V rapids. But first-timers like Mike probably grappled with an intense fear of the unknown. As we pulled into the McKay Hydro Station on the west branch of the Penobscot River, I glanced over at him; he looked terrible. Will he go through with it? I wondered.

A group of boisterous young men hooted and hollered as they exited the bus. Their paddles hoisted overhead, they seemed eager and ready to battle the river.

Not Mike. He was still tense and silent.

Our raft was parked at the top of the Ripogenus Gorge. We could hear the powerful, rushing water long before we approached the edge. The deep canyon was lined with fifty-foot granite walls for the first 300 yards.

"Not a place you want to fall out," someone said. "No shore to swim to. The only way out is to ride the rapids."

Just then Nick, the rafting company's videographer, pointed to a huge rock down river. "I'll be filming you guys from right over there," he said. "That's right, I'll be catching your terrified faces as you fly out of the raft and plunge into those rapids of mayhem!"

Mike looked like he was about lose his breakfast.

"Okay, okay," our guide interrupted. "Everyone, get your raft and follow me."

We carried ours to the launching spot just upstream from the dam responsible for the monster rush of white water. Right after we put in, the guide explained a few simple but important commands before she asked us to practice.

"All forward!" she barked, watching as we paddled in almost-unison.

"All back! All back!"

We back-paddled furiously.

"Okay, good," she said in her normal voice. "Once we steer the raft past the dam, we'll hit the first class five rapid—also known as 'Exterminator Hole'—in about forty seconds. If we make it through without flipping, don't take a vacation, because we hit 'The Staircase'—that's another class five—immediately after it."

"Yeah baby!" someone shouted.

"Yeah, it's awesome! Just make sure you don't celebrate after that first rapid or we'll get nailed on the second one. You guys ready?"

Five rafters shouted at once: "Let's go!" "Yeah!" "Ready!"

Mike gripped his paddle fiercely and nodded.

"Okay then, let's do this!"

I counted down in my head. Forty, thirty-nine, thirty-eight, thirty-seven...

Our speed increased.

Twenty, nineteen, eighteen...

We surged past giant boulders. The rapids were in sight.

Five, four, three...

"All forward!" the guide shouted. "Faster! Faster!"

Bam!

We dropped into a hole of mayhem at full speed and hit a wall of water full on! The rubber raft seemed to bend in half. A nanosecond later, I felt the icy water's ferocious impact. WAHOO!

"Forward!" the guide roared.

Adrenaline gushed through my veins as I paddled furiously. The raft dropped down again, and water pummeled us from all sides. But we made it! Whooping it up, we high-fived with our paddles.

"Holy crap!" Mike exclaimed. "I can't believe we just did that!"

"Pretty amazing, right?"

He grinned and nodded. His once-taut face had finally relaxed.

We had more river to paddle, though nothing like those Class V rapids. And before we knew it, the field trip was over.

After his day on the river, Mike started running marathons (talk about crazy!), participating in triathlons (talk about hard!), and doing stand-up comedy (talk about brave!).

He was living out of his skin—undaunted and unbounded.

Invitations for challenging field trips will come your way. Take a page from Mike's playbook—say yes and ignore the naysayers in your head as well as your life. Lean into adventure that lets you discover just what you're capable of!

Go white-water rafting!

DISCLAIMER: If you have a medical condition, consult your physician before participating in any physically demanding activities. Beginners, of course, should try easier rapids before attempting more challenging ones.

Field Trip Challenge: After you get your feet wet, try a rafting adventure with more exhilarating rapids!

Suggestions for white-water rafting field trips around the country:

NORTHEAST

Maine: The Kennebec, Dead, and Penobscot Rivers are a paddler's delight! Raft all three.

Call-To-Action Plan:

1. Find a rafting trip that suits your adventure level. If you're not an adrenaline junkie, opt for waters with Class II or III rapids.

2. Invite friends along.

3. Research whether you'll need to rent a wet suit.

4. Enjoy the thrills!

5. Do a post field-trip review.

Massachusetts: The Deerfield River in the Berkshires has up to Class IV rapids (Charlemont).

Pennsylvania: Raft either the Lehigh River in the Pocono Mountains (Weatherly) or the Youghiogheny River ("Yough" to locals) in Ohiopyle State Park.

MIDWEST

Wisconsin: The Menominee River has Class IV and V rapids during the spring season (Athelstane).

SOUTHEAST

Georgia: The Toccoa River in the Chattahoochee National Forest (McCaysville) is a great place for families.

North Carolina: Try the Nantahala River for Class II and III rapids (Bryson City).

Tennessee: The Ocoee River has two sections: the lower one (Pigeon River) is great for beginners, and the upper section (Hartford) has Class III and IV rapids for those who want a bigger thrill.

West Virginia: Check out New River Gorge and Gauley River for more challenging rapids (Lansing).

SOUTHWEST

Arizona: Raft the Colorado River through the Grand Canyon (Flagstaff).

New Mexico: Find great rafting adventures near Taos Ski Valley on the Rio Grande and Rio Chama (Taos).

WEST

California: The South Fork of the American River offers a wide variety of rafting opportunities (Lotus and Coloma).

Colorado: Head to the base of Mt. Evans and raft Clear Creek (Idaho Springs) or the Arkansas River (Canon City or Buena Vista).

Idaho: Try the Salmon River for Class II and III rapids (Stanley).

Montana: You can't raft in Yellowstone Park, but you can raft along its border on the Yellowstone River (Gardiner). Or check out the Gallatin River near Big Sky.

Oregon: Beginners can test the waters at Hellgate Canyon on the Rogue River. More advanced rafters will prefer Nugget Falls (Merlin).

Wyoming: The Snake River has views of the Grand Tetons as well as great white-water rafting or scenic float trips (Jackson Hole).

35

Forty-eight Mountains

've always hiked around the country whenever I could. Hiking is not only a great form of exercise, it connects me with nature, gives me time to reflect, and often changes my perspective for the better. But I had never set myself a hiking challenge.

After a fourth basketball concussion, however, my doctor suggested I give up contact sports, so I started looking for another activity to keep me fit. About that time, my siblings and I were visiting Mom at her New Hampshire timeshare. We decided to hike Mt. Eisenhower, a 4,780-foot member of the Presidential Range. Three-quarters of the way to the summit was a large, yellow park service sign:

STOP
**THE AREA AHEAD HAS THE
WORST WEATHER IN AMERICA.
MANY HAVE DIED THERE FROM EXPOSURE,
EVEN IN THE SUMMER.
TURN BACK NOW IF THE WEATHER IS BAD.**

Lucky for us, the weather that early October day was sunny and warm. We made the summit without any problems and enjoyed spectacular views of autumn's October Glory. I had so much fun, I wondered if hiking might make a good substitute for basketball. Maybe I could tackle the rest of the Presidential Range.

But that sign made it clear I'd have to change my casual approach. I was used to taking off in a pair of sneakers with a backpack borrowed from one of the kids. The White Mountains required more thorough preparation and respect. I didn't know it then, but I'd already learned my first mountain lesson: **Take warning signs seriously!**

I started working on my Presidential-Range goal late the following summer. With improved footwear, I set out to conquer the summits of Jackson and Pierce with my friend Gregg. It was a wet day, and when I hurried over what looked like a flat rock, my feet came out from under me. I crashed-landed on my elbow and sliced my hand. **Mountain lesson #2: Give slippery downhill-facing rocks the respect they deserve.** Thankfully, Gregg was both a Boy Scout leader and a veteran, so he had **come prepared with a first aid kit—Mountain lesson #3.**

But not all the lessons that day were harsh. I saw one of the famous White Mountain huts where day hikers can refill water bottles and distance hikers can get a bed, a hot dinner, and a hearty breakfast. **Mountain lesson #4: Hiking can be enjoyed on so many different levels!**

I had notched two more presidential peaks on that hike; I had only six more to go. But then my daughter Caitlin asked me to join her on a trek up Cannon Mountain. It isn't part of the Presidential Range, but it is one of New Hampshire's forty-eight 4,000-footers. Summitting the forty-eight is a popular goal for serious hikers. In fact, those who achieve it can join The AMC Four Thousand-Footer Club, which now has over 14,000 members.

Hmmmm, I thought. *Bigger challenge. Way more field trips. Entry to AMC's exclusive club.*

I was now in hot pursuit!

SCOTT'S SURPRISE

A week after adding Cannon to my summit collection, my brother Scott asked me to hike Mt. Monadnock in Southern New Hampshire. Though not part of the White Mountains or a 4,000-footer (it's just over 3,000 feet), Monadnock is the second-most hiked mountain in the world after Japan's Mt. Fuji. For me, it's a great place to train when time or conditions put The Whites out of reach.

Scott hadn't hiked since Mt. Eisenhower, so like many of Monadnock's daily visitors, he stopped frequently to rest and catch his breath. Seeing him struggle, I urged him to turn back, but he wouldn't. When we made the summit, he vowed to be in better shape for the sibling hike during our annual trip to Mom's timeshare.

That weekend, he surprised me. "Let's do Washington!"

"Washington!" I exclaimed. "That's the biggest, baddest peak in the Northeast!"

Mt. Washington's 6,288 feet might not sound impressive—especially to people who live near the Colorado Rockies—but some of Earth's fastest wind speeds and deadliest weather have been recorded there. In Not Without Peril, Nicholas Howe tells stories of people who lost their lives on that mountain.

"The weather will be perfect tomorrow," Scott insisted. "I'm up for it if you are."

"Okay, let's do it!"

We set off on the Ammonoosuc Ravine Trail. My brother had made good on his promise—he was in better shape—but when we reached the Lake of the Clouds, an AMC hut just a few miles from the summit, he sat down for a rest. I had a goal to chase, so I dashed over to

Mt. Monroe. We continued to Washington's summit together when I returned.

At last, we stepped out of the wilderness and onto the "rock pile" at the mountain's top, but instead of seeing a few scattered hikers, we saw hordes of tourists. They had either driven up the auto road or taken the Cog Railway. They, too, wanted to see the magnificent views and stand in the place Native Americans would never go, as they regarded it as the Great Spirit's home.

Imagine—a mountain that has taken so many lives is now easy for everyone to access.

No matter how they arrived, those who stood on top of New Hampshire's highest peak looked out on breath-taking wilderness with mountains in every direction. The Presidential Range spanned from north to south, the Carter Moriah Range rose up out of the east, and Vermont's Green Mountains stretched along the west. Some peaks seemed close enough to reach on a short walk, but Scott and I knew better. After taking one long, last look, we found the trail and headed back down the mountain.

Thanks to my brother, I bagged the hardest peak at the beginning of my field-trip challenge. Six mountains down, only forty-two to go!

THE DECISION

Weather and timing didn't always align, so I didn't return to the White Mountains until the following August.

When I started out from Massachusetts with friends Gregg and Babu, bright sun had already heated the summer day to eighty degrees. But in New Hampshire's Franconia Notch two-and-a-half hours later, clouds covered the mountains and the temperature had dropped to the forties.

Mountain lesson #5: Check the mountain forecast— hour-by-hour temperature, wind, and precipitation reports that let hikers cancel if they're not prepared for challenging weather.

Had we known conditions were wet and cool, we would have stayed home or dressed more appropriately. But we decided to hike anyway.

Despite the cool temperature and misting rain, my body heated up quickly. Though sweating in my short-sleeved shirt, my arms were cold to the touch. Back then, I didn't understand the importance of regulating body temperature in the mountains. I didn't know people died from hypothermia—even in the summer.

Hypothermia happens when your body loses heat faster than it can produce it. You may not realize your temperature is dropping because the rigorous workout makes you feel hot. Being wet makes you even more vulnerable, so controlling sweat and staying dry are essential to survival when temperatures grow colder closer to the summit. Yet there I was, sweating in cold, misty conditions, unaware of this very real and potentially deadly danger.

Mountain lesson #6: Wear layers, and always carry a towel to dry off and an extra base layer to change into after summiting. It'll keep you warm.

Luckily, the temperatures didn't drop more that day. But when the Madison Spring Hut appeared on the trail, I was happy to dry off and warm up with a bowl of potato leek soup. I checked the map and saw we were only four-tenths of a mile from the summit. Finishing should be easy, I thought.

But when we set out again, the atmosphere was as dense as the soup we'd just eaten. After hiking another two-tenths of a mile over large, jagged boulders, we realized visibility was down to about five feet. We didn't want to become one of the 2,000 hikers who wander off the trail and get lost every year. Nor did we want to risk injury from a misstep. So, just two-tenths of a mile from the top, we made the proudest decision hikers can make: We turned back.

Mountain lesson #7: The mountain will always be there to hike another day. Don't let the summit's lure cloud your judgment.

Gregg, Babu, and I didn't notch Madison that day, but we still earned a badge of honor. The mountain had tested our judgment, and we'd made the right decision.

THE GIFT

I was determined to tackle as many of those forty-eight summits as time would allow, so eight days later, I stood on top of Mt. Isolation with my friend Mark.

Pointing to the Presidential Range, I said, "There's Madison—the one we couldn't summit last week."

"Is that Madison or Adams? I know they're right next to each other, but which is which?"

"Not sure."

At that moment, a young hiker from Maine popped up.

"There's an app for that," he said. "It's called 'PeakFinder.' If I hold my phone over the view like this, it tells me what I'm looking at."

"Cool! That's a must-have hiking tool!" I exclaimed. "Thanks for taking the time to show us."

"Sure," he said, and continued on his way.

What a gift! My family and I have used that app countless times, and I've shared it with numerous other hikers on the trail.

Mountain lesson #8: Endurance exercise, mountain serenity, and cool technology are a hard-to-beat combo!

SCRAMBLING

In early September, Mark and I tackled Mt. Adams, a 5,774-foot peak in the Presidential Range.

The trail we chose required a lot of scrambling—using both hands and feet to climb over boulders or up rock formations. It's where the hiking and rock-climbing worlds meet.

Grading systems help hikers determine every trail's level of difficulty on a scale of one to five, one being straight hiking and five involving rock climbing with ropes. The steep boulder field Mark and I climbed was probably a two. Still, it was dangerous and required careful footing and strenuous hoisting. When we finished, we both felt like we had beat a worthy opponent. What a great field trip within a field trip!

After Adams, we topped off the day by "peak-bagging" Mt. Madison—the mountain I'd almost summitted with Gregg and Babu. "Peak-bagging" means collecting multiple peaks in one hike. It's a strategy used by those determined to get through the forty-eight.

Mountain lesson #9: It's easy to find additional field-trip challenges in the mountains!

SOLO

Hiking alone feels different for everyone. Some find it peaceful; others get a little anxious. I'd hiked Monadnock solo, but since 342 people swarm the mountain's 1,000 acres every day, others are around to help if you get hurt—and they inevitably scare off the wildlife. After hiking it over 100 times, I've only seen a grand total of two porcupines and one deer.

The White Mountains, on the other hand, span 800,000 acres. That's a lot of
wilderness! You're more likely to encounter bears, moose, and wild cats. Hiking alone, I wouldn't have a buddy like I did back on the golf course in Banf. I'd be the only option on the menu! But if I wanted to finish the forty-eight in the next year, I had to get used to going by myself.

For my first solo in the Whites, I planned to climb Mts. Lincoln and Lafayette, so I arrived at the trailhead at 5:30

a.m. to get an early start. Unsettled by the dark and the empty parking lot, I stayed in my car for what seemed like five minutes to contemplate my first step.

"Let's do this," I finally said out loud.

Outside the car, the light from my headlamp lit a path to the trail, and I stepped into the wilderness. The sun came up about ten minutes later. The sight and sound of waterfalls along the route soothed me, and I saw other solo hikers on the summit of Mt. Lincoln. Now I know hiking alone is pretty common in the White Mountains.

After peak-bagging Lafayette, I felt what I usually feel after pushing myself to a great limit—incredibly alive! In fact, I was so totally exhilarated, I ran the four-mile Bridle Path Trail back down the mountain. WAHOO!

My first solo field trip in the Whites had put me on cloud nine!

TOO MUCH

Five days later, I invited my colleague Rob—an active hockey player in good shape—to join me on a trek up Mts. Flume and Liberty. But I miscalculated what an athlete without mountain experience could accomplish.

The average hiker takes about one hour to cover two miles, plus an additional hour for every 1,000 feet of elevation.

We set out on a ten-mile hike that gained 3,677 feet, so Rob faced a challenging eight-hour workout. That would have been hard enough by itself, but the trail I chose also included steep slides—rock face requiring serious hand-over-hand scrambling.

"If you don't feel comfortable climbing up the slide, you can opt out," I told Rob before we started. "The trail description says there are bailouts through the woods."

Rob attempted the first scramble but used the bailouts for the rest. Even so, he needed to rest constantly to catch his breath and frequently stumbled on the descent.

"My legs feel like Jello," he told me.

I knew what he was talking about. Hiking down the mountain puts enormous pressure on the quads and knees—more so than uphill.

By the time we reached the parking lot, he was ragged. He'd tried to do too much too soon. For him, the hike was more torture than fun. I worried his experience would keep him off the mountains in the future.

Mountain lesson #10: Make sure hiking companions know what they're getting into! Match field-trip challenges to experience level, so folks enjoy their time in the mountains and want to come back for more.

BUSHWHACKING

Mark and I hiked the North and South Twins in mid-October. As we approached the first summit, we saw a truly beautiful sight—snow crystals sparkling among the fall foliage. That was another first—I'd never been on top of a snow-covered mountain before.

We also peak-bagged Mt. Galehead and faced a dilemma: retrace our steps or hike along the road? Neither option seemed appealing, and both would make our hike longer.

Mark pulled out his phone to look at Google Maps. "We could bushwhack through the forest and connect to a snowmobile trail," he suggested. "That'll take us back to where the car's parked."

I looked at the map. "I've never bushwhacked before, but it sounds better than the other two options. Let's do it."

Thanks to technology, we made it back before dark and kept the hike to nineteen miles—the most I'd ever completed in the Whites.

"Firsts" and "mosts" seemed to happen on every hike. The mountains always showed me something new!

ICE

People I met on the trail would tell me how great it was to hike in winter. While I've always liked hiking, I never even considered doing it in the snow and ice. But I had a goal and didn't want winter to stand in my way, so I acquired crampons and traction cleats for ice, and snowshoes for deep snow.

I packed the traction cleats for a late-October hike up Mts. Tripyramid North and Middle. Sure enough, the trail was slick with a thin layer of ice. Time to try out the new equipment. What magic! Those little contraptions let me crunch up the big slide like a mountain goat.

Then the left set broke off right in the middle of the steep trail. Are you kidding me?! I thought. Now what? Get microspikes, said the voice inside my head. Yeah, right— as soon as I get down this mountain.

With one mountain-goat foot and a normal one, I maneuvered from side to side, grabbing onto trees to pull myself up. Slowly and carefully, I made my way to the summit. By then the sun had melted the south slide. Thank goodness I wouldn't need traction for the descent!

That day, the mountain took it easy on me.

On another hike to the Garfield summit, Mark and I saw a group trying to descend a snow-packed slope without any traction. They simply could not stay standing. Arms flailed as people fell and slid down the mountain. Fortunately, only their pride was hurt, but had they broken a bone, their descent would have been excruciating. In some conditions, it could have been deadly.

The image of those hikers—and my own equipment failure—stayed with me. When faced with an icy scramble on Monadnock without crampons, I turned back.

Weeks later, I saw a trio of young men slipping at that same spot now covered in hard, thick ice. "Do you guys have traction with you?" I asked.

"Nah," one said. "But we'll be fine."

"Just remember it'll be harder to descend without it," I warned. But they kept going.

Just remember, there's no shame in climbing back down and returning more prepared on another day. In fact, it's the more honorable choice when faced with such formidable conditions. The mountain always wins—especially if you don't take its lessons to heart.

SNOW

Snowshoes didn't seem appealing. The thought of hiking through snow with an extra four pounds strapped to my feet seemed harder, not easier, so I avoided using them. But after a few minutes of comically sliding down one very steep slope, I finally gave in. The results weren't magical because I kept tripping. "It'll be midnight before I get off this mountain," I muttered.

Eventually, I got used to the snowshoes and even noticed how the televators—bars that elevate the heels—cut down the steepness and gave me an edge. Okay, I thought, these things do make a difference.

Nevertheless, hiking in snow is definitely harder because every step requires twice the effort. Without a goal to reach, I might not have attempted it. But then I wouldn't have seen the beautiful snow-covered trees along the trails or the gorgeous snow-capped mountains from the summit. And I never would have experienced the intentional butt slides, like the one I took on the Hancock Loop Trail. One half-mile, tree-lined section has a chute with a seventy-one percent grade. Sliding down that mountain luge track made me feel like a kid again!

Then there was the utterly phenomenal cloud inversion I witnessed from the summit of Starr King. A cloud inversion happens when the air below is cooler than above, creating a sea of clouds. The sight was so magnificent, I did something I rarely do—I sat down in the snow and just stared.

Mountain lesson #11: Winter hiking is totally worth the extra effort!

FORREST GUMP

Matt, a new hiking buddy I met on the Zealand Bond Traverse, had agreed to join me for the eighteen-mile trek up Owl's Head. At the top, we talked with a mother and her adult son.

"You guys chasing the forty-eight?" the son asked.

"Yes," I said. "This is my forty-sixth."

"Last week, I met a guy who quit hiking after his forty-seventh mountain. Can you imagine?"

"He sounds like Forrest Gump," I observed, referring to the movie character who ran for three years until he suddenly stopped and said, "I'm pretty tired. I think I'll go home now."

We all chuckled. But honestly, I felt like Forrest.

Owl's Head had been my fortieth New Hampshire summit in less than a year— a number that didn't include hikes in other states. On top of that, I biked hundreds of miles in the summer heat to stay in shape.

After the eighteen-mile trek to Owl's Head, I was bone-tired but had already prearranged to hike Mt. Cabot with Gregg the next day and Mt. Moriah with Scott the day after.

Should I cancel?

But you're so close to your goal, my better angel urged. The weather looks good, and you already have two able partners lined up. I trudged on but afterward was grateful both Gregg and Scott had driven to and from the mountains for those hikes because I was physically exhausted—something I wasn't used to.

But after a three-day vacation from exercise, I was ready to get number forty-eight!

THE LAST PEAK

People who hike the forty-eight select their last peak for different reasons. Some choose Bondcliff because its rocky overhang provides the best photo op. Some pick Mt. Isolation because it's a long hike with no opportunities for peak-bagging. Others leave Owl's Head for last because it's an eighteen-mile slog for an unremarkable peak.

I saved Jefferson—a summit on the Presidential Range.

Mark joined me for this special hike, which seemed right because he shared the most peaks with me. We hiked at a similar pace, but when necessary, we took turns pushing each other.

My brother Scott hiked the second-most peaks with me, and even though he couldn't join me that day, he was with me in spirit—as were all my other hiking companions. Babu, Gregg, Rob, Caitlin, and my new friends Matt and Nicole—who I met during solo hikes—had all been part of my pursuit of the forty-eight.

While that quest seemed to be the number-one priority, a huge bonus was connecting with people. At first, I'd send out a blanket text asking if anyone wanted to hike. A few friends would regularly say yes and then people started texting me with hiking invitations. As I met new folks on the trail, my hiking network expanded.

Friends in Facebook groups provided good information about trails, cheered on fellow hikers, and celebrated every summit—but none more than the forty-eighth. I was already looking forward to posting a summit photo of me holding the bright pink #48 sign Helen made me.

On the trail, I told Mark my legs still felt tired and a little sore even after a three-day rest. That wasn't unusual. I'd been racing against Father Time and the normal muscle atrophy that comes with age. It was a race I couldn't win, but at least I slowed that old codger down, and that felt really good!

When Mark and I finally reached the summit, I looked out over Mt. Washington and the other Presidentials. Their majestic beauty seemed even more spectacular knowing I had stood on top of each one. They had challenged me physically, mentally, and emotionally, and I was enormously grateful for every hard-earned lesson and reward.

Those mountains had packed a ton of learning in every field trip!

On the hike down Castle Trail, my chocolate, hazelnut, and marshmallow sandwich tasted sweeter than usual and my legs didn't seem as sore. As my energy perked up, I started pondering a new question: What's the next field-trip challenge, Jay?

You still need to finish the Whites' Terrifying Twenty-Fives, I told myself. Then you have just ten peaks to notch the New England Sixty-Seven.

But enough about me! What about you?

The mountains are waiting... gear up and get out there! Find your hike—one where you can succeed and return safely—and spend time with Mother Nature and other special friends.

FIELD TRIP:

Take a hike!

Field Trip Challenge: Set a goal to hike some number of trails in a year. Start with flat rail trails and slowly progress to hikes involving more elevation and miles. Tackle challenging hikes only when your cardio is in good shape and your legs can handle the descent.

Call-To-Action Plan:

1. Review the gear list below and make sure you're properly equipped.

2. Research a hike that suits your physical condition.

3. Invite a friend!

4. Check the weather and set a date.

5. Savor the wilderness beauty all along the way!

6. Do a post field-trip review.

HIKING TIPS:

1. Eating. I don't like to eat in the middle of a strenuous workout, yet I need calories for energy. To solve this problem, I eat breakfast before leaving my house and another meal (usually a tuna or smoked salmon sandwich) right before the hike. My pack also has trail mix in one outside pocket and fruit in the other. If I get moderately hungry on an ascent, I reach for the fruit. If I feel like I'm hitting an early wall, I break out the trail mix for salt and protein. For the descent, I pack my favorite trail sandwich—a s'more-like concoction of chocolate hazelnut spread and marshmallow crème.

2. Drinking. It's hard to consume enough water, but if you don't, you'll likely feel it later that night. Keep water containers on the outside of your pack to make staying hydrated easier.

3. Safe River Crossing. Unbuckle your pack so it doesn't act like an anchor if you fall in.

WHAT TO WEAR:

1. Trail runners. This sneaker-like footwear works best in anything but snow or ice.

2. Winter hiking boots. My Oboz boots keep me warm in below-zero temps, repel snow and water, and provide great traction.

3. Smartwool socks. Far better than cotton socks, these stay dry even in the summer.

4. Water-resistant outer layer. Useful for wind and rain protection.

5. Down outer layer. Necessary for winter hikes. Mine folds into its own pocket.

6. Layers. In winter, I usually hike with an Under Armour base layer, a moisture-wicking tee shirt, and a quarter zip.

7. Pants. Single-layer lightweight pants or shorts work best on warm days. Lined pants are great for the cold.

8. Hats. A breathable, vented baseball hat keeps bugs, spider webs, and other problems out of my eyes and the sun off my face when above tree line. In cold weather, I start with either a fleece-lined or lighter-weight beanie and switch to a baseball hat as my body temperature increases.

9. Backpack. My Osprey has a vent field on the back to keep my back cooler and dryer.

WHAT TO CARRY IN OR ON THE PACK:

YEAR-ROUND ESSENTIALS:

1. Water. Carry one liter for every two hours on the trail plus a little more in case you get stranded on the mountain. If you're hiking near a stream, pack a water filtration system instead of bottles.

2. Gatorade. Most of the time, I don't drink the one bottle in my pack, but if I'm putting in heavy miles, I like to replenish electrolytes.

3. Food. Bars, trail mix, fruit, and sandwiches all work.

4. Extra socks. Wet feet cause blisters, which hurt and make hiking unpleasant.

5. Lip gloss and sunscreen.

6. Sleeping pad and bag. For added warmth or sleeping in emergencies.

7. Headlamp and extra batteries. Useful if dark descends before you're off the mountain.

8. Tissues: Handy for sinus issues and going to the bathroom in the woods.

9. First-aid kit. BAND-AIDS, bacitracin, etc.

10. Moleskin. Pack pre-cut pieces in case of blisters.

11. Multi-purpose tool. For cutting and other unforeseen uses.

12. Portable phone charger.

13. Mobile phone. For Alltrails, Google Maps, and PeakFinder apps. The Pro edition of AllTrails costs $29 per year and lets me download the trail map and access it without cell coverage. This valuable tool helps me know if I've accidently left the trail and gives me peace of mind in the wilderness.

14. Map: I take a picture to look at on my phone and also keep a hard copy in my pack.

15. Emergency blanket pack. These foil-based blankets take up very little space, weigh only a few ounces, and preserve body heat during an emergency.

16. Bug net. Weighs nothing and keeps bugs from bothering you.

17. Bug spray. I don't carry it, but many hikers do.

18. Bear spray. A pepper spray to ward off dangerous wildlife.

19. Trekking poles. Useful for support on descents and to aid traction in winter.

WINTER/FALL ESSENTIALS:

1. Crampons. Provide traction on ice.

2. Micro spikes. For traction in packed snow and light-ice surfaces.

3. Snowshoes. Get the ones with the televators!

4. Goggles. Useful on extremely cold days.

5. Leg gaiters. Wrap these over your boots to prevent the snow from going inside.

6. Hand and foot warmers. Use these with mittens so they work quicker and help you avoid frostbite.

7. Gloves and mittens. Keep an extra set along with mittens in the pack. If everything gets wet, use the extra socks to keep your hands warm and dry.

8. Glacier glasses or sunglasses. Winter solar glare can cause big problems if your eyes aren't protected.

9. Koozies. These keep water bottles from freezing and preserve your phone's battery.

10. Gaiter. Face covering for extremely cold days.

11. Ice axe. Useful for self-arrest and provides grip in icy conditions.

Disclaimer: Choose a hike appropriate for your level of fitness, and if you have health problems, talk to your doctor before heading out.

SUGGESTIONS FOR HIKING FIELD TRIPS:

NORTHEAST

Connecticut: Mt. Frissell. For a three-state hike, park in Massachusetts and take the 2.3-mile Mt. Frissell Trail that gains 800 feet of elevation. Summit in Massachusetts then walk a few hundred feet to the Connecticut high point. To set foot in New York and get a picture with the tristate marker, take the five-mile Mt. Frissell and Brace Mountain Loop.

Delaware: Walking Dunes Trail at Cape Henlopen State Park (Lewes). This 2.6-mile loop gains only fifty-nine feet. Extend your hike by connecting with a short trail to the beach.

Maine: Blueberry Ledges Trail in Baxter State Park (North of Millinocket). Maine has many great trails, but I picked this one because I love Baxter State Park. This eight-mile, out-and-back trail gains 994 feet and might lead to a moose sighting!

Massachusetts: Wachusett Summit Loop at Wachusett Mountain State Park (Princeton). This 4.9-mile hike gains 1,151 feet. On a clear day, you can see Boston— 44 miles away as the crow flies.

New Hampshire: Mt. Morgan and Mt. Percival Loop (Center Sandwich). This 5.5- mile, moderate loop gains 1,535 feet. Mt. Morgan has ladders, small tunnels, and some hand-over-hand climbing. Percival also has hand-over-hand climbing and tunnel-like spaces between rocks. If this sounds fun, enjoy! For a tamer trail, cross the street and hike West and East Rattlesnake Mountain via Old Bridle Path. The 3.1-mile, out-and-back hike gains 853 feet. Both hikes have great views of Squam lake.

Differently abled folks who want to experience summit views can take the Cannon Ski Area's tram to the summit of Cannon Mountain. Or join other tourists on Mt. Washington's auto road or the Cog Railway.

New Jersey: Monument Trail Loop at High Point State Park (near Wantage). This 3.5-mile trail gains 515 feet and produces two rewards: great views and a picture at the state's highest point.

New York: Bear Mountain Loop Trail in Bear Mountain State Park. Only 50 miles from New York City, this 3.8-mile loop gains 1,154 feet. It's a great place to train for the next-level hike.

Pennsylvania: Appalachian Trail, Pinnacle Trail, Valley Rim, and Pulpit Rock in Berks County Park (near Hamburg). This 9.1-mile loop gains 1,236 feet. See great views of the Lehigh Valley and tell folks you hiked on the Appalachian trail!

Rhode Island: Cliff Walk (Newport). This 6.6-mile, out-and-back trail gains 324 feet and is a Newport must. Admire rocky coastline on one side and spectacular mansions on the other. The trail is paved, except for a short section where you walk on big, flat, easy-to-navigate rocks.

Vermont: Keewaydin Trail to Overlook Spur via Long Trail in Okemo State Forest. Hike another Appalachian Trail section on this 3.4-mile, out-and-back trail that gains 1,210 feet and features a waterfall, beautiful vistas, and boulder scrambles.

MIDWEST

Illinois: Starved Rock State Park (Oglesby). Choose the 2.5-mile French Canyon Trail or the 4.3-mile Starved Rock and Sandstone Point Overlook to see eagles.

Indiana: Turkey Run 3, 10, 9, 5 Trails Loop in Turkey Run State Park (Marshall). This loop covers four trails and 3.9 miles and gains 521 feet.

Iowa: Pleasant Creek Lake at Pleasant Creek State Recreation Area (near Shellsburg). This 8.6-mile loop gains 626 feet.

Kansas: Prairie, Gas House, and Davis Trail Loop in the Tallgrass Prairie National Preserve (New Strong City). This 8.4-mile loop gains 541 feet. The preserve protects the remaining four percent of the tallgrass prairie that once spread across the Midwest. View the herd of Tallgrass Prairie bison reintroduced back in 2009.

Kentucky: Van Hook Falls and Cane Creek Valley in Daniel Boone National Forest (near London). I just had to choose a Daniel Boone hike! This 5.7-mile, out-and-back trail gains 626 feet and has a waterfall.

Michigan: Mt. Arvon (near Michigamme). Hike to the state's highpoint on this 11.2-mile, out-and-back trail gaining 951 feet.

Minnesota: Oberg Mountain Loop via Superior Hiking Trail (near Tofte). A 2.6-mile loop that gains 521 feet. Hike it twice if you feel good! Beautiful views of Oberg Lake and Lake Superior.

Missouri: Lewis and Clark Trail and Lewis Trail Loop in Weldon Spring Conservation Area (near St. Charles). This 7.1-mile loop gains 859 feet and passes by limestone cliffs and bluff escarpments with views of the Missouri River.

Nebraska: Oak Creek Trail (near Brainard). This 12.8-mile, point-to-point trail only gains 160 feet, but it's great for putting on miles and seeing wildlife. Either car spot* or go as far out as you wish to come back.

Ohio: Ledges Trail at Cuyahoga Valley National Park (near Hudson). This 2.6-mile trail only gains 154 feet. Add additional trails in the network to get a longer workout.

Oklahoma: Turkey Mountain Via Yellow Trail (near Tulsa). Just ten minutes from downtown, this 3.7-mile loop gains 377 feet, offers views of the Arkansas River, and connects with other trails.

Wisconsin: Devil's Lake Loop in Devil's Lake State Park (near Baraboo). This 4.7-mile loop gains 997 feet— a big gain for Wisconsin! That might explain why more than three million people visit the park annually.

* "Car spotting" means you and your companion both drive to the end point, drop one car, then drive back to the beginning point together. Reverse the process when you finish the hike.

SOUTHEAST

Alabama: Kings Chair Loop in Oak Mountain State Park (Pelham). Only 21 miles from Birmingham, this 4.2-mile trail gains 734 feet.

Arkansas: Falls Branch Trail in Lake Catherine State Park (near Hot Springs National Park). This 1.6-mile loop only gains 213 feet, but it crosses Little Canyon Creek several times and eventually ends up at a scenic waterfall on Falls Creek.

Florida: Florida Trail Segment: Clearwater Lake to Alexander Springs in Ocala National Forest (near Astor). You'll need to car spot to hike this 10.6-mile, point-to-point trail that gains 249 feet. Shade isn't abundant but wildlife is.

Georgia: Stone Mountain Walk-Up Trail (near Atlanta). One of the most popular hikes in the Atlanta area, this 2.2 mile, out-and-back trail on smooth granite gains 567 feet.

Louisiana: Longleaf Vista Road to Backbone Trail in Kisatchie National Forest (near Mora). This 10.6-mile loop gains 646 feet and has a little bit of everything, but one downside—the last two miles are on the road.

Maryland: Grist Mill, Sawmill Branch, Santee Branch, Cascade Falls, Ilchester Trail Loop in Patapsco Valley State Park (near Baltimore). This 8.7-mile paved loop gains 1040 feet.

Mississippi: Bear Creek Outcropping Trail in Tishomingo State Park (near Dennis). This 3.6-mile loop gains 259 feet and winds through massive rock formations and fern crevices in the Appalachian foothills.

North Carolina: Crabtree Falls Trail Loop (near Marion). Find the trailhead on the Blue Ridge Parkway close to Pisgah National Forest, the hiking epicenter of North Carolina. Explore many other hiking options when you've finished this 2.6-mile loop, which gains 577 feet and rewards you with Crabtree Falls.

South Carolina: Sassafras Mountain to Pinnacle Lake at Table Rock State Park (near Sunset). Car spot for this point-to-point trail. If you start at Sassafras Mountain—the highest point in South Carolina—and end at Pinnacle Lake, you'll hike 9.1 miles, gain 980 feet, and see waterfalls. If you reverse the hike, you'll gain at least three times the elevation.

Tennessee: Virgin Falls Trail in Virgin Falls State Natural Area (near Pleasant Hill). This 8.3-mile, out-and-back hike gains 1,305 feet. You'll walk down to the falls then gain all the elevation when you climb back up.

Virginia: Crabtree Falls Trail in George Washington and Jefferson National Forests (near Tyro). Another Crabtree Falls trail! This 3-mile, out-and-back trail gains 1,102 feet and features a waterfall.

West Virginia: Seneca Rocks Trail in Spruce-Knob Seneca Rocks National Recreation Area. I love this area! Once you see Seneca Rocks, you'll totally want to hike it! This 3.2-mile, out-and-back trail gains 800 feet. While there, enjoy the Monongahela National Forest.

SOUTHWEST

Arizona: Cholla Trail on Camelback Mountain (Paradise Valley). The easiest—and busiest—way up the mountain, Cholla Trail gains 1,161 feet over the 2.6-mile round trip and rewards you with fantastic views of the valley. For more elevation, take Echo Canyon Trail and gain 1,423 feet over the 2.4-mile, out-and-back hike. Afterward, head down the street to Pizzeria Bianco, one of the best pizzerias in the world. You've earned it!

New Mexico: Picacho Peak Trail in Santa Fe National Forest (near Santa Fe). This 3.3- mile, out-and-back trail gains 1,227 feet and offers panoramic views of the National Forest and Santa Fe.

Texas: Lost Mine Trail in Big Bend National Park. This 4.2-mile, out-and-back trail gains 1,099 feet and serves as a great warm-up for bigger climbs at Big Bend. Enjoy views of Casa Grande as well as Pine and Juniper Canyons.

WEST

Alaska: Thunderbird Falls Trail (near Chugiak). Only 26 miles from Anchorage, this out-and-back hike is only 1.8 miles and gains 301 feet.

California: San Clemente Beach Trail (southern California). A 4.5-mile walk along the ocean—what more can you ask for? In northern California, head to Muir Woods Trail in Muir Woods National Monument (Mill Valley). I absolutely love this place! The 2.2-mile loop gains only 144 feet but meanders through magnificent redwood trees.

Colorado: Deer Mountain Trail in Rocky Mountain National Park. With gorgeous views of Longs Peak, Moraine Park, and Upper Beaver Meadows, this 5.6-mile, out-and-back trail gains 1,400 feet to the 10,013-foot summit. If you're still adjusting to the higher altitude, save this trail until you acclimate. Instead, hike Bear Lake Nature Trail also at Rocky Mountain National Park. This 0.7-mile trail circles the lake and gains only forty-two feet. Get there really early to beat the crowds.

Hawaii: Diamond Head Summit Trail (Oahu). This 1.8-mile, out-and-back trail gains 452 feet, has a fascinating history, and boasts 360-degree views of the island and the Pacific Ocean. Puu Poa Beach (near Princeton, Kauai). See beautiful views of Hanalei Bay as you gain 200 feet on this 1.6-mile, out-and-back trail. Kilauea Iki Trail in Volcano National Park (Big Island). On this 4-mile loop, gain 400 feet then descend through a rainforest to a solidified yet still-steaming lava lake. Supply Trail in Haleakala National Park (Maui). The round trip is only 4.6 miles and gains 975 feet. Arrange to ride a bike down the mountain road for an extra field trip!

Idaho: Mineral Ridge National Recreation Trail (near Coeur d' Alene). This loop covers 2.9 miles, gains 649 feet, and has beautiful lake views.

Montana: Mount Sentinel via Hellgate Ridgeline in K Williams Natural Trail Area (Missoula). This 3.1-mile out-and-back trail is a must! Gain 1,896 feet and enjoy views of Mount Jumbo, Rattlesnake National Recreation Area, and the Bitterroot Mountains. If the summit is too much, stop at the famous "M" created in 1908 by University of Montana Forestry club members. Students forged a zigzag trail and carried stones to shape the university symbol. From the "M," see all of Missoula as well as the university, Clark Fork River, and distant mountains.

Nevada: Turtlehead Peak Trail at Red Rock Canyon National Monument (near Las Vegas). A favorite hike just 20 miles from Vegas, this 4.6-mile, out-and-back trail gains 1,988 feet and has tremendous views of the city's neon lights and the park's red rocks.

North Dakota: Caprock Coulee Loop in Theodore Roosevelt National Park (near Watford City). This loop gains 524 feet over 3.8 miles and has stunning views of the Little Missouri River. Keep your eyes open for bison!

Oregon: Misery Ridge and River Trail at Smith Rock State Park (near Terrebonne). Smith Rock State Park is in the high desert, so it's different from the hiking in Oregon's other national forests. This 4-mile loop gains 1,043 feet and lets you glimpse golden eagles, prairie falcons, mule deer, river otters, and beaver.

South Dakota: Main Street to Sheridan Lake Section of the Flume Trail in Black Hills National Forest (near Rapid City). A relic from the 1880's mining days, this 12.4-mile, point-to-point trail gains 1,351 feet and mostly follows the flume bed.

Utah: Bald Mountain Trail in Uinta-Wasatch-Cache National Forest (near Kamas). While this out-and-back trail is only 2.6 miles, you gain 1,145 feet in 1.3 miles—that's a lot for beginners. Since the summit is nearly 12,000 feet, altitude may also be a challenge. Take it slow! If it's your first high-altitude hike, bring a small can of oxygen in case you need a hit. Amazing views of the surrounding alpine lakes await you at the top!

Washington: Twin Falls Trail in Olallie State Park (near North Bend). This 3.6-mile out-and-back trail gains 967 feet. Enjoy both the upper and lower falls.

Wyoming: Cascade Canyon Trail in Grand Teton National Park (near Moose). This popular 9.7-mile, out-and-back trail gains 1,128 feet. Arrive early—you'll need to take a boat across Jenny Lake to get to the trailhead. See great views of Hidden Falls and look out over the park from Inspiration Point.

36

Bucket List

O nce you've finished a massive field-trip challenge, there's only one thing to do—examine your bucket list and start another one!

I never even thought about a bucket list until asked to share mine at a Chamber of Commerce event. I didn't have one. But soon after, I read a magazine article about a woman who hiked the highest points of all fifty states. That sounded cool, and only 315 people had ever done it. Fewer than 650 had summited highpoints for the forty-eight contiguous states. Compare that with the more than 4,500 people who've climbed Mt. Everest. By the end of that article, I had a bucket list and a plan to join the Highpointers Club.

Unlike AMC's Four Thousand Footers Club, Highpointers not only lets you join at the beginning of your quest, it allows you to design your own challenge. Some people climb only the mountains they'd enjoy, while more serious hikers scale the most formidable peaks—like Denali or Mt. Rainier. Since it doesn't matter if you drive or hike to the marker, others might stick to the places accessible by road, like Mt. Washington. My goal was to stand on all the highpoints in the continental U.S.—hiking when possible, driving when necessary—and for me, joining the club was like announcing that intention to the world. Now I had to get the list done!

I was excited to discover I had already notched three of the forty-eight highpoints. My family had hiked Vermont's Mt. Mansfield (4,393 feet) years ago. After every rafting adventure on the Penobscot River, I usually hiked Maine's Mt. Katahdin (5,268 feet) and, as recounted in the previous chapter, I climbed New Hampshire's Mt. Washington (6,288 feet) with Scott.

Only forty-five highpoints to go!

My new list clawed at me, but work, family, friends, and other responsibilities made it challenging to find highpointing time. Where could I extend work travel or fit work around my expeditions? How could I involve friends and family? Which adventures would need to be solo? How much of the country could I see up close and personal?

The list was a new kind of mountain to climb. And you already know how I feel about mountains. The field trips! The astounding views! The opportunity to do and see more!

Come along with me on some of my highpointing adventures. I hope they inspire you to create your own field-trip challenge!

MORE NEW ENGLAND HIGHPOINTS

My next highpoint hike was in my home state. Like several others across the country, Massachusetts's Mt. Greylock (3,491 feet) has a mountain road so anyone can drive to the summit, but I preferred to reach the top on foot.

That October, I was still chasing New Hampshire's forty-eight, but the Whites were already packing snow. I wasn't yet an experienced snow hiker, so I asked Scott to join me for a hike up Mt. Greylock. We ascended via the Bellows Pipe Trail and enjoyed great views of the town and the surrounding hills. On the descent down the Thunderbolt Trail, I found myself looking back and thinking, "This would be a blast to ski." Scott and I ended the pleasant fall excursion with a stop at Jaeschke Orchards for apples and cider donuts. Yum!

Six days later, I zipped over to Rhode Island's Jerimoth Hill (812 feet), the closest highpoint to my home. You can make this flat, easy walk an adventure by combining it with outings to the Roger Williams Zoo, Scarborough or Misquamicut Beach, Newport's mansions and the famous cliff walk, or the Tennis Hall of Fame. For a festive evening, schedule a visit when Providence hosts WaterFire, an outdoor event where the city lights torches in the river that flows through its center. Grab a bite at Al Forno, the home of the original grilled pizza, and stroll among the fun vendor booths along the river.

Without wandering far from home, I had easily crossed off two highpoints. Where to next? Only forty-three possibilities remained!

THREE HIGHPOINTS, TWO BROTHERS, ONE GREAT DAY

Scott agreed to join me for an early November hike up Connecticut's Mt. Frissell (2,380 feet), which spans three state borders and sits near a must-see fifty-nine-foot waterfall. (See "Suggested Field Trips" in the previous chapter for trail details.) We hiked the five-mile loop and grabbed a cool picture at the tristate marker (MA, NY, CT).

Afterward, we drove over to New Jersey's Highpoint State Park (1803 feet) for another relatively easy hike. The Monument Loop Trail is only 3.5-miles—perfect for new hikers and children to enjoy summit views of Pennsylvania, New York, and New Jersey and the 220-foot high War Veteran's Monument.

"Wanna grab another highpoint?" I asked Scott.

"How far is it?"

"Three hours."

"Why not?!"

It was dark by the time we arrived at Delaware's Ebright Azimuth (448 feet).

"We're in the middle of a neighborhood," Scott observed. "And it's utterly flat."

"Yeah, well, not every highpoint involves a climb. Let's get the photos and leave before we cause too much disruption."

Though hardly memorable in itself, the destination inspired an impromptu road trip remarkable for its simple pleasures: stunning foliage along back roads, great sandwiches from the local WAWA—the area's legendary convenience store—and best of all, time with my brother.

I had collected eight highpoints, but they were all within relatively easy reach. Now I'd have to book flights, hotels, and rental cars. With one great road trip and some cool discoveries under my belt, I felt prepared to take highpointing to the next level!

AN EYE-OPENING FATHER-SON ROAD TRIP

December business meetings in Florida triggered a hankering for more field trips. With a little bit of planning, I could visit Biscayne National Park, spend time with my son Kevin, and knock off a few southern highpoints.

With business and Biscayne in the rearview mirror, I picked Kevin up at Orlando's airport and drove 405 miles north to Florida's Britton Hill (345 feet). Smack dab in the middle of farm country sits Paxton's Lakewood Park; the highpoint marker, where we snapped a few pictures, is only a thirty-yard walk from the parking lot.

"I can't believe we just drove all that way to photograph a marker in a small-town park," Kevin remarked.

"We're exploring new territory. Without the highpoint quest, what reason would we have to drive through small, southern towns? We're seeing a part of America we wouldn't otherwise see. Isn't that cool?"

"Since you put it that way, yeah, I guess it is," Kevin agreed as we started the two-hour drive to Montgomery, Alabama.

The historical landmarks from Montgomery's ugly past left an everlasting impact on us both. We started at The Legacy Museum located on the site of a former warehouse where Black people were held before being sold into slavery.

Equally powerful was the nearby National Memorial for Peace and Justice, a sacred place commemorating the victims of lynching. Suspended from its ceiling are multiple steel columns representing countless lost lives. Looking at them, I had the same gut reaction to racial terrorism as I felt standing on the USS Arizona in Pearl Harbor—the horror of it all sickened me.

We left Montgomery feeling chilled by its inhumane past but impressed by the city's efforts to confront it, and we talked about it all through the two-hour ride to Alabama's Cheaha Mountain (2,407 feet).

The drive—like the conversation— became more interesting, too. After hours of straight, flat roads, we finally hit curves and hills closer to the park. But then the signs to Cheaha disappeared at the same time as our cell signal. We were in the middle of nowhere, with no one to point us in the right direction.

The experience taught us three valuable lessons:

1. You can't always rely on technology.
2. Always bring paper maps.
3. Don't exit out of the GPS app. If you keep it going, it'll keep you in tune with your directions. But if you shut it down, all bets are off.

After a few wrong turns, we finally made it to the trailhead and enjoyed the hike up the mountain. The panoramic views of the Talladega National Forest were so beautiful, we ate lunch at the summit's Vista Cliffside Restaurant. The restaurant and lodge are accessible by a mountain road, so anyone can enjoy being on top of Alabama.

After a day of history and hiking, Kevin and I needed a different kind of field trip. In Birmingham—our last Alabama stop—we enjoyed a fun evening at Top Golf, which is a cross between a driving range and a bowling alley. Kevin loved it so much, we've since enjoyed this activity in several other cities.

The next morning, we started our day at the Birmingham Zoo before driving to Mississippi's Woodall Mountain (806 feet). On the way, we stopped at a southern institution—Waffle House—so Kevin could experience this classic chain known for abundant, inexpensive food and its family-friendly vibe. The line cooks were a hoot—they kept us chuckling.

Woodall Mountain in Luka, Mississippi sits on land owned and used by a gun club, so we drove to its summit to avoid stray bullets, took the requisite photos, then headed to Memphis, Tennessee.

In Memphis, we ate at a great place—Rendezvous Barbecue—and Kevin gave it the best review a restaurant can ask for: "I could eat this every day," he said, licking his fingers.

Afterward, we watched the Miami Heat basketball team slay the Grizzlies at the FedEx Forum then grooved to the Blues on Beale Street. On day two, we visited the National Civil Rights Museum at the Lorraine Hotel where Dr. Martin Luther King was assassinated.

"I always admired Dr. King," I told Kevin. "I wish I'd had the opportunity to meet him. His 'I've been to the mountaintop' speech—the one he delivered the day before he was assassinated—still sends chills down my spine every time I hear it."

On Martin Luther King Day, Kevin called me from school.

"Dad, thank you for bringing me on that highpointing trip," he said. "Those Civil Rights Museums really opened my eyes, and now I have a much better understanding of racial inequality."

Talk about a highpoint....

As this trip confirmed, the "list" is so much more than scaling a peak or collecting marker photos. It's an opportunity to learn about other places and people, experience new flavors and food, and create wonderful, life-changing family memories.

WILD PONIES, COAL COUNTRY, AND MORE

By March, I was ready for another highpointing excursion. My friend Mark and I flew to Atlanta for a six-state hiking trip.

Despite pouring rain, we headed straight for Georgia's Brasstown Bald (4,784 feet), hiked the short trail to the summit, then did the Arkagoah Trail before driving to Cherokee, North Carolina.

"Awesome!" I exclaimed as we pulled into the hotel parking lot. "We're right across the street from Harrah's Casino!"

"You planning to gamble?" Mark asked.

"Nope. I'm just excited because it means we're close to great food!"

Early the next morning, we headed for Smoky Mountain National Park and picked up the Appalachian Trail at Newfound Gap for our hike to Tennessee's Clingmans Dome (6,643 feet). The auto road was still closed, so only hikers could reach the Dome's observation tower and enjoy astounding views of the Smoky Mountains stretching for miles. By the time we finished the nearly 16-mile hike on that rollercoaster-like trail, I was already longing for dinner at Ruth's Chris Steakhouse.

On the way out of the park, we got an unexpected treat: a herd of about thirty elk roamed the fields near the Oconaluftee Visitor Center. Remembering that Banff wildlife specialist who warned about charging elk, I made sure to keep my distance!

Mark and I left early the next morning for Ashville and drove to North Carolina's Mt. Mitchell (6,684 feet). Though a road allows anyone to reach the highest peak on the East Coast, we hiked the Mt. Mitchell Trail in the Pisgah National Forest, a gradual 5.6-mile ascent loaded with switchbacks. Then we trekked the 1.5-mile Deep Gap Trail over to Mt. Craig, the second-tallest East Coast mountain.

Mark and I enjoyed the mountain drive to Virginia. He is the absolute best navigator; when the directions are always spot on, the only responsibility left is to enjoy the great company, the beautiful scenery, and the awesome hikes!

At Grayson Highlands State Park, home to Virginia's Mt. Rogers (5,729 feet), we hiked the ten-mile Rhododendron Trail from Massie Gap to the Appalachian Trail then the short spur to the summit. The rugged highlands reminded me of Scotland, but the absolute stars of the show were the wild ponies. They're so used to humans, they don't even bolt if you walk by them.

After Mt. Rogers, we drove nearly three hours to Kentucky's Black Mountain (4,145 feet) to notch one more easy highpoint. Since it's owned by a coal-mining company, you can't hike to the summit, but you can drive up a cool mountain road—most of which is in Virginia—and walk the short distance to the Kentucky marker.

Coal country was new to me. I was shocked at seeing a mountain's side blasted off but still interested to watch the coal industry at work.

On the drive back to our home base, I was already thinking about dinner. "Hey Mark, is Johnson City, Tennessee anywhere near our route?"

"Yes."

"Then we have to eat at Ridgewood Barbecue. Their pit beans are fantastic!"

The beans and pulled-pork sandwiches were as good as I remembered—and a worthy reward after a long day of hiking. Don't miss this great food if you're in the area!

The next day, I dropped Mark off at the airport in Charlotte, North Carolina and picked up my new road-trip partner—Helen! We wanted to watch Kevin's college baseball team play a few spring games. When he had a late afternoon game, we took a morning drive to the summit of South Carolina's Sassafras Mountain (3,553 feet) and did a short hike. Being with Helen made that highpoint extra special.

After enjoying Kevin's games, we toured Congaree National Park with him. What could be better than family, baseball, national parks, and highpoints? And speaking of highpoints, I now had seventeen. WAHOO!

PITTSBURGH PIZZA, AMISH COUNTRY, AND WEST VIRGINIAN GEMS

Attending my son's baseball games is a priority, so it was tough to fit highpointing in during baseball season. But I formulated a plan and even got Scott to join me. After picking up the rental car in Pittsburgh, we tackled our first goal—deciding once and for all on our favorite Pittsburgh pizza. In the Squirrel Hill neighborhood, I grabbed a pie from Aiello's and Scott got one from Mineo's. We savored both pizzas on the way to Pennsylvania's Mt. Davis (3,212 feet) but still couldn't decide which was better.

For a couple of guys from Massachusetts and Connecticut, seeing Amish country and its horse-drawn buggies was really cool. On Mt. Davis, we hiked four trails and found the woods oddly quiet—no people, bird, or animal sounds. At the top of the summit's seven-flight observation tower, we saw 360-degrees views of the Forbes State Forest and the

Negro Mountains, a long ridge of the Allegheny Mountains.

The day was still young, so we drove to Maryland's Backbone Mountain (3,360 feet), passing through Silver Lake, West Virginia, home of the very cute "smallest church" and the "smallest mail office." The round trip to the highpoint is only 2.2 miles, so we had extra time to explore part of the Monongahela National Forest until our empty stomachs urged us to seek dinner at the Gateway Restaurant in Riverton, West Virginia. When we arrived late at the Smoke Hole Cabin Resort, the check-in clerk had left instructions for getting into our room. "It'll be open," the note said.

The resort is laid out like a roadside motel where the rooms are open to the outside. Scott and I didn't know what to expect from our room or the several people sitting on the front porch. Turns out, they were a cool group of motorcyclists from Michigan who returned to this part of the country every year. And sure enough, our room was open. Nothing like an easy check-in for two tired hikers!

On the way to West Virginia's Spruce Knob (4,863 feet) the next day, Scott and I returned to the Gateway Restaurant to load up on biscuits with gravy and pancakes with applesauce. After the six-mile hike to the summit, we were rewarded with views of the Monongahela National Forest and the George Washington and Jefferson National Forests in Virginia.

On our flight back to Boston, Scott said, "That was an epic trip!"

It was! Without the highpointing list, we never would have glimpsed Amish culture, seen the beautiful Monongahela Forest, or experienced rural America's warm hospitality.

With three more highpoints, I now had twenty down—only twenty-eight more to go!

MOUNTAINEERING ON MT. HOOD

Thanks to a late June wedding in White Salmon, Washington, I had a great reason to visit the Northwest and nab Oregon's Mt. Hood (11,239 feet).

Helen, Kevin, and I arrived in Portland and were instantly stunned by the view of Mt. Hood—an absolute beast still covered in snow. When we reached the legendary Timberline Lodge—6,000 feet up on the mountain's shoulder—a June snowstorm blew in our faces.

Though nowhere near the tallest highpoint, Mt. Hood is both a volcano and a glacier, so it's a serious challenge. Climbing it would be my first foray into mountaineering—next-level hiking that requires special equipment like ropes, harnesses, crampons, and ice axes. I'd used crampons and an ice axe in the White Mountains but never had to worry about avalanches or falling into a crevasse—let alone inhaling sulfur fumes from a dormant volcano. Plenty of people have died climbing Mt. Hood, so I hired Timberline Guides to assist with my first mountaineering trek.

I met my guide Jeff the following day. He made sure I had the proper clothing and equipment then taught me some mountaineering fundamentals, like how to use ropes for climbing and an ice axe for self-arrest. Soon we were off to the Silcox Hut, where we had dinner with the twenty-three other hikers and caught a little shut-eye before our 2:00 a.m. start time. That's right—to ensure the ice ledges are still frozen when you pass by, you have to start hiking Mt. Hood in the middle of the night.

I admired the night sky's sparkling stars and steered clear of the fumaroles venting hot, sulfurous gases. When daylight appeared around 4:45 a.m., the rising sun cast the mountain's shadow down on the landscape below. What an utterly glorious sight! We took celebratory pictures with the Cascade Mountain Range in the background then beelined back to the Silcox Hut for my third breakfast of the day—delicious waffles.

Mountaineering success plus family time plus wedding fun equaled one incredible field trip!

THE HIGH PLAINS

Highpointing is fascinating—in one state, you scale a glacier, but in another, you simply drive a long way to step on a single plot. That's what I did to bag Nebraska's Panorama Point (5,424 feet).

While attending a conference at the Gaylord Rockies Resort in Aurora, Colorado, I noticed a four-and-a half-hour window between sessions—just enough time for the round trip to Panorama Point.

Driving through Pawnee National Grassland made me wish I'd given myself more time to explore the internationally renowned birding location. Though I spied a coyote and some mule deer in the beautiful grasses, with another two hours, I could have taken the self-guided tour on its many birds and their habitats.

Panorama Point is on private land owned by the family that operates Highpoint Bison Ranch. A long dirt driveway cuts through fields dotted with bison and mule deer and ends at the highpoint marker. Though it's over 5,000 feet and known as Constable Mountain, Panorama Point is flat as a pancake—a mere low rise on the high plains.

Without a highpoint marker, few people would visit the vast, open plains. But I'm glad I did. It helped me appreciate how huge and geographically diverse America really is.

COLORADO'S ALTITUDE CHALLENGE

After the conference, I planned to climb Colorado's Mt. Elbert (14,433 feet)—a tough highpointing challenge for a guy from low-lying Massachusetts.

My hometown near Boston is only about 700 feet above sea level—a long, long way below Elbert's 14,000 feet. To avoid acute mountain sickness, I'd have to give my body time to increase its red blood cells, which is how it counteracts the decreased air pressure and lower oxygen levels at high altitudes. If I didn't, I could get very sick on the climb and possibly even die.

Spending time at the Gaylord acclimated me to 5,000 feet, but I needed to get used to much higher elevations. So, as a next step, I hiked Flattop Mountain's 12,324 feet. To guarantee the trek went well, I rested when necessary and moved at a more cautious pace.

My daughter Michaela joined me for the rest of the trip, and we did a few hikes in Rocky Mountain National Park, took a guided horse ride, then drove up the scenic Trail Ridge Road. That little jaunt gave me two days over 12,000 feet. On the way back to the hotel from the park, we stopped for the best thing I ate on the whole trip—cherry pie at the Colorado Cherry Company in Lyons. That pie is a worthy destination all its own—don't miss it!

We drove to Leadville, Colorado, so I could sleep at 10,000 feet the night before the highpoint hike. A guy at the local bike shop offered a great tip: "Bring a can of oxygen. It weighs nothing, and you can take a hit if you find yourself out of breath."

Five minutes later, a can was stowed in my pack.

I was at the trailhead by 5:30 a.m. so I'd be off the summit by noon—a strategy advised by experts to avoid getting caught in the massive afternoon storms so common on fourteen-thousand footers.

Even though I'd trained for it, the altitude made the hike challenging. At 12,000 feet, I started taking shorter steps to keep my breathing under control. Fifteen hundred feet later, I used some canned oxygen. Did those few hits make a difference? I don't really know. But the deep breath I took afterward made me believe it did.

About four hours from the time I left the trailhead, I stood on the summit admiring the gorgeous view of the

Rocky Mountains and nearby Mt. Massive. My endorphins in full bloom, I felt fantastic! Not only had I notched a tough highpoint, I had just hiked the second tallest mountain in the continental United States!

My highpointing adventure over, Michaela and I headed to Aspen, a beautiful town framed by breath-taking mountains and filled with high-end boutiques and restaurants. "Now this is my vibe," she said.

From there, we explored more of Colorado's spectacular wilderness like Black Canyon of the Gunnison National Park—a mini–Grand Canyon. On our way back to Denver, we drove through Grand Mesa and White River National Forests then stopped for Rocky Mountain pizza at one of my favorite Denver-area restaurants—Beau Jo's at the base of Mt. Evans in Idaho Springs.

Back in Denver, it was my turn to help Michaela with her own bucket-list challenge. She wanted to attend a game at every Major League Baseball stadium, so we headed to Coors Field to see the Colorado Rockies play the Cincinnati Reds.

"Dad, good call on the itinerary," Michaela said as we toughed out a two-hour rain delay. "At first I was bummed we weren't planning to spend more time in Denver. It's a cool city, but it can't compete with the Rockies, Black Canyon... or Aspen. Thanks for an awesome trip."

Who'd have thought a rain delay would lead to another Rocky Mountain high!

Before our flight home the next evening, I wanted to squeeze in Kansas's Mt. Sunflower (4,039 feet), so I left the hotel at 6:00 a.m. and drove three-and-a-half hours to another middle-of-nowhere destination. Like Nebraska's highpoint, "Mount" Sunflower is on private land (though the owners encourage visitors) and is indistinguishable from the surrounding pastures. My ride to and from Denver was a study in massive hay, wheat, and corn fields, and not much else.

But those scenes—and others from the trip—evoked the familiar lyrics:

Oh, beautiful for spacious skies, For amber waves of grain, For purple mountain majesties Above the fruited plain! America! America!

Oh, beautiful indeed! High on that great feeling, I realized Mt. Sunflower put me halfway to my goal. Twenty-four highpoints down—just twenty-four more to go!

ADIRONDACK DISCOVERIES

Though seemingly smaller than Nebraska's Panorama Point (5,424 feet), New York's Mt. Marcy (5,344 feet) is an actual mountain; on the seven-mile hike to the summit, you gain 3,513 feet. At Panorama Point, you don't gain any. Numbers don't always tell the whole story!

The four-hour drive to the Adirondacks took me through the Berkshires of western Massachusetts and New York's Lake George—both beautiful places. When you get close to Lake Placid, ski jumps rise high above the trees and look strangely out of place in summer's greenery.

I did my usual drop-the-bags-at-the-hotel routine then went next door to the Lake Placid Olympic Center. Standing where the "Miracle on Ice" took place, I relived the U.S.A.'s historic gold medal win against the Finnish hockey team during the 1980 Olympics. All through dinner that night, I remembered the country-wide celebrations.

Early the next morning, my friend Matt joined me for the 14.1-mile hike. Even though the trail's surfaces seemed easier to walk on than those in the White Mountains, Matt—who has climbed New England's sixty-seven peaks in hiking sandals—sustained a toe injury. But he kept trekking, and over the course of our hike, we talked about highpointing. He, too, thought it was a cool challenge and has since taken it up.

Highpoint number twenty-five introduced me to the Adirondacks' forty-six 4,000 footers. The lure of another hiking list makes upstate New York an area I want to return to!

SCARY SOLO HIGHPOINTING MOMENTS

Eager to make more headway on my list, I set off on a solo trip to visit two national parks and three highpoints—Oklahoma, New Mexico, and Arizona. I flew into Denver and immediately set out for southern Colorado's Great Sand Dunes National Park. Those dunes are not only the tallest in the country, they were a lot of fun to hike, even with the forty-mile-an-hour winds throwing sand everywhere.

After an overnight at the Fairfield Inn in Alamosa, Colorado, I headed to the first highpoint, Oklahoma's Black Mesa (4,973 feet). Neither a car nor a human was in sight when I pulled into the trailhead's very rural and isolated parking lot. Looking out over the flat, barren land with mesas—flat-topped hills bounded by steep escarpments—I tried not to think about the mountain lions, bears, and rattlesnakes spotted here over the past few weeks. I focused instead on the soothing sight of cattle grazing on the plains. Surely, a mountain lion would prefer those cows to skinny old me! But I was still spooked by the thought of getting bitten or attacked, so I hiked the eight-mile trail in just over two hours then high-tailed it out of there!

The ride to Taos Valley Ski Area in New Mexico took me through beautiful desert plains with red-rock mesas, but I couldn't enjoy it. I was too stressed out by my nearly empty gas tank. I had originally planned to get gas on the way to Black Mesa, but my GPS took me around the town. No problem, I thought, I'll get it on the way out. But then the GPS took me through nothing and past nowhere!

Now I was about 130 miles from Taos Valley with forty miles of gas left. I saw signs for Folsom, New Mexico and, assuming it must have a gas station, traveled over nineteen miles of dirt roads to get there. Turns out, Folsom has a post office and a museum (which was closed)—but no gas. Spying a truck next to the post office, I headed inside, hoping to find someone to help me.

Lucky for me, the young lady said I only had to drive eight miles west to Des Moines.

Jay, I thought, always carry a map. If I'd had one, I could have avoided all those dirt roads! When my tank was at last full, I finally relaxed and enjoyed the rest of the ride.

After overnighting at the Blake Hotel in Taos Ski Valley, I found not a single soul at the trailhead for New Mexico's Wheeler Peak (13,161 feet) when I arrived at sunrise the next morning. I know this is starting to sound like a thing, but this time, I didn't have to worry about being eaten. It was cool—not unsettling—to have the forest to myself and see all the non-life-threatening wildlife out and about.

A mile from the summit, concerns about altitude sickness kicked in, so I slowed my pace, kept my steps deliberate, and inhaled some oxygen. Clearing a ridge, I hit almost fifty-mile-per-hour winds for the first time. But shielding my eyes and angling into those gusts, I pushed through and made it to the summit where the temperature had dropped below thirty degrees. The extraordinary views made it all worth it.

On the way down, I eventually ran into groups of people, including some senior hikers who had wandered off the trail. I told them about the pro version of the AllTrails App, which allows for tracking without mobile coverage, giving me confidence to hike the mountains alone.

Coming out of the forest to the site of Bavarian Haus, I rewarded myself with a delicious apple strudel on their sun-bathed deck. Then it was back to the hotel before the long drive to Albuquerque on the way to Arizona.

Arizona's Petrified Forest National Park was full of highlights: The Painted Desert, Blue Mesa, Puerto Pueblo, Jasper Forest, and the Crystal Forest. If you're ever in that area, make sure you hit every single one!

A day later, when I hiked Arizona's Humphreys Peak (12,633 feet), the forest portion was great. I had to do some scrambling in the mountain's saddle—the low point between two ridges—and took a shot of oxygen around 12,000 feet. The summit was a happening place with a bunch of hikers already there, and I could see why—the top-down view of the Grand Canyon was awesome.

On the way down, I met many friendly people, including a group of young professionals I'd chatted with at the trailhead that morning. The Arizona hiking community made me feel like I was among friends, which made my solo hike that much more enjoyable.

But when I returned to my rented Volvo, the humor began.

Somehow, when I put my pack in the car's hatch, I accidently popped the safety lock off my bear spray and doused myself. Yikes! Once my car aired out and I could breathe, I beelined back to the hotel. Racing against check-out time, I showered quickly then jumped back on the road toward Phoenix to catch a flight home that evening.

Before long, my body felt like it was on fire. Maybe it's the hotel shampoo, I thought. Sometimes those tea tree shampoos make your head tingle. But this was much more than a tingle and it wasn't just on my head. The underside of my wrists—the area hit directly by the bear spray—felt hot and so did other areas of my body. It can't be the bear spray, I told myself. Unless...

Concerned about what, exactly, I had on my skin, I called my best resource: Helen. She jumped on the computer for some quick research.

"Bear spray has cayenne pepper in it," she said.

"How do you get rid of it?"

"Wash with dish soap for twenty minutes."

"Great. I guess my five-minute shower didn't do the trick."

"It also says you can easily spread the oil to other parts of your body."

"Fantastic... I probably did that when I toweled off."

Needless to say, my ride to Phoenix was a hot one!

But I still had to stop for some of the country's best pizza at Pizzeria Bianco. Later that night, my flight was canceled. Normally, that would have been a bummer, but now it meant booking a hotel room and getting that cayenne pepper off sooner rather than later!

Bear spray and all, it was a great trip. In one year, I had brought my highpoint total to twenty-eight and my national park total to eighteen. Not only did I see much more of our vast and geographically diverse country, I lived to tell the tale!

CANYONS, CAVERNS, AND SAND-SLEDDING

With the highpoint list still clawing at me, I planned another trip about a month later. November seemed like a good time to hike Texas's Guadalupe Peak (8,749 feet), so I invited my daughter Caitlin and her fiancé Bryan to join me for a southwestern road trip.

After flying into Austin, we had a seven-and-a-half-hour drive to The Lajitas Golf Resort, a cool place with the feel of an old western town. Its breakfast patio looked out on Big Bend National Park and the Mexican mountains across the Rio Grande.

In Big Bend, we sat in the hot springs and visited the Santa Elena and Boquillas Canyons then drove to the artsy town of Marfa. The next day, we stopped at Guadalupe Mountains National Park to familiarize ourselves with the highpoint's trailhead then feasted on garlic knots and salmon with Creole sauce at the Trinity Hotel in Carlsbad, New Mexico. That meal was so fantastic, we returned again the next evening!

The following morning's weather was perfect as we hiked Guadalupe Peak and enjoyed the fall colors still in full bloom. At one point, the 4.2-mile trail lined with various trees made me feel like I was in a forest; elsewhere, the Prickly Pear Cactus gave it a desert feel. On the summit, I looked down on El Capitan—obviously not the famous rock formation in Yosemite National Park but Texas's tenth-highest peak.

"Hey Dad, guess what?" Caitlin asked as she and Bryan met me at the top. "Only two guys passed us on the way up—you and another guy!"

"Yeah, and we blew by a ton of people," Bryan added.

"Awesome, guys! Proud of you!" I grinned. "You've made great time!"

Before heading back down the mountain, I took one more longing look at El Capitan's layered summit. I would've loved to hike it, but that wasn't in the cards because we had other fun planned: Carlsbad Caverns National Park, an overnight at the Springhill Suites in Las Cruces, and sledding down the dunes at the White Sands National Monument (now a national park). All the fun of snow sledding without the cold!

By the time we headed home, I'd snagged my twenty-ninth highpoint, visited three national parks and one national monument, and—most importantly—spent time with Caitlin and Bryan.

One list—so many awesome field trips!

THE PANDEMIC PAUSE

The Texas trip took place in November 2019. By February 2020, COVID-19 had started spreading in the United States, forcing me to forego highpointing until a vaccine makes travel safe again. Until that time, I'll keep busy finishing off the White Mountains' Terrifying Twenty-Five Trails and hiking the New England Trail, a 215-mile path that starts at Long Island Sound and winds across Connecticut and Massachusetts.

Whenever we get the all-clear, I'll be ready to climb the remaining tough highpoints—California, Idaho, Washington, Wyoming, Utah, Montana, and Nevada—as well as those in the remaining midwestern and southern states.

Having these lists keeps me focused on doing the things I love and does wonders for my physical and mental health—especially now.

What do you love doing? What's your plan for maximizing your fun time?

If you don't know, there's no time like right now to figure it out. So, get busy and be ready. You won't want to waste a second!

FIELD TRIP:

Create your own bucket-list adventure!

Call-To-Action Plan:

1. Ask yourself, "What places do I want to see? What experiences do I want to have?"

2. Create your own list that'll challenge you to see and do as much as possible.

3. Invite friends along!

4. Record your adventures in a journal or a photobook.

5. Finish the challenge—then create another one! Or even better, have multiple lists going at the same time, like I do!

Suggestions for Field-Trip Challenges: Visit all sixty-three national parks.

"Collect" as many waterfalls as you can. Start with all falls over a certain number of feet in your state and then advance to other states.

Hike a long-distance trail like the Appalachian Trail on the East Coast, the Pacific Crest Trail on the West Coast, or the Continental Divide Trail. Together, they're known as the "triple crown of hiking."

Visit all the botanical gardens or arboretums across the U.S.

See a game in every stadium for your favorite sport.

Create your personal golf-course bucket list and play on each one.

Attend a game/competition in every major sport.

Drive all seventy interstate highways within the continental U.S.

Photograph every lighthouse in the U.S.

Visit all the fine art museums in every major U.S. city.

Tour all fourteen presidential libraries.

Walk every street in your town.

Epilogue

Years ago, I supervised a group of middle schoolers on a hike up Wachusett Mountain. Beforehand, I asked the teacher if I could lead the faster group of students.

The day of the hike, my group ran up the mile-long trail in no time, admired the view for a few minutes, then sprinted back down, passing all the other groups still going up.

When the teacher saw us, she bellowed, "Mr. Hummer—slow down! Slow down!"

I'd heard that command my whole life.

As we sped by her, I yelled, "Some things never change!"

What about you? Have you changed? Has your adult life squelched your inner child? Visit everydayisafieldtrip. com for more inspiration!

Check out our bucket list ideas, photos, videos, and more. Become part of our community of adventurers, explorers, and curiosity seekers! Share your field-trip photos and join me in inspiring others to get out there and have fun!

See you out there!

Acknowledgments

When I returned home from chaperoning my son's school trip, my lovely bride Helen asked, "How was the field trip?

"It was great, but you know, every day is a field trip."

I stopped and thought about what I'd just said. Was it true? I felt sure, but to be certain, I decided to keep a log of my daily field trips. After about six months, I realized that I do indeed live my life as if every day were a field trip.

I shared my findings with Helen. Over the course of our discussion, we both came to realize that if Jay from the neighborhood could live that way, then anyone could choose to live a more fulfilling life, every day.

I knew I wanted to share that message with others, but I didn't start writing *Every Day Is A Field Trip* until after I was downsized from my corporate executive position. So, the first acknowledgement goes to the company that set me free. Thank you for giving me the opportunity to create a book that will, I hope, help others develop a mindset for having fun every day.

My greatest thanks and appreciation go to Helen for having faith in me and for taking this life-long journey together. Thank you for your patience and for being the most radiant, nicest person I know. You are more than I ever dreamed of.

The "Every Day Is A Field Trip" concept came from my Mom who always encouraged me to find joy every day. That wasn't always easy for a single parent raising five kids, but my Mom pulled it off. She was and is an amazing woman. Mom, thanks for being greater than you know!

Caitlin, Michaela, and Kevin, my three children, not only supplied me with many field trips over the years but continue to inspire me by living their best lives each day. Thanks for staying true to you, and yes, thanks for the field trips, including when you "take Dad out for a walk." Special thanks to Michaela and Caitlin who, after reading an early draft, sought out new adventures described in the book. This led me to hope other readers will be inspired to pursue field trips they otherwise may not have considered.

I met Kate Early, my editor, when I was recruiting her son Jake to play on my high-school showcase baseball team. Talk about a big recruiting moment! I not only had success recruiting a great player, but his dad Mark coached the squad with me, and afterward became one of my best hiking partners. When Mark, Kate, Helen, and I were out for pizza one night, and Kate mentioned her writing work, I had one of those "aha" moments—I had found the person to make sense of my book! Kate, thanks for the many hours you put into *Every Day Is A Field Trip*, so I could share the movement with the world. It was truly a pleasure.

Thank you to my sister Dawn, who agreed to read an early draft of the book as if it hadn't been written by her brother. Your comments—"this is fun" and "I never thought of doing that field trip"—made me believe that *Every Day Is A Field Trip* could help people live a more fulfilling life.

A big thank you to Jule design for creating a fun book jacket design and our *Every Day Is A Field Trip* Logo. I love them both.

To my many friends, family members, and colleagues mentioned in the book (even if your name was changed to protect the innocent), thank you for being involved in my life and for providing great stories and memories by the bucketful. I could not have enjoyed life to the fullest without you.

About the Author

Former corporate executive, baseball coach, field-trip chaperone, nature lover, theater-goer, music fan, and experience collector, Jay Hummer has spent a lifetime blurring the boundaries between work and play. An avid fun-seeker since childhood, he figured out early how to capitalize on opportunities to do the things he loves: play sports, eat good food, connect with people, and see the world. As a successful franchise-business corporate executive, he traveled throughout the U.S. and Europe exercising his yen to explore in his free time.

Now a successful entrepreneur, the author continues to fit in fun and discovery around work and family life wherever and whenever he can. From his home base in Massachusetts, he, his wife Helen, and their three grown children still take frequent field trips to literally climb new mountains, explore unvisited vistas, or just gaze at marvelous sunsets from one of the thousands of picturesque locations across America.

His new mission is to get 'folks' to stop limiting play to weekends and vacations and incorporate it into every possible moment.

EVERY DAY
is a
FIELD TRIP

**If you enjoy taking field trips, join our
EVERY DAY IS A FIELD TRIP COMMUNITY:**

Visit us at
www.everydayisafieldtrip.com
to read our blogs, see our products,
and find more field trip opportunities.

Made in the USA
Columbia, SC
04 May 2021